New Light
on
New Testament
Letters

New Light on New Testament Letters

Clifford A. Wilson M.A., B.D.

Director, Word of Truth Productions Ltd.

Formerly Director of The Australian Institute of Archaeology

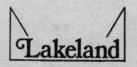

LAKELAND
BLUNDELL HOUSE
GOODWOOD ROAD
LONDON S.E.14

ISBN 0 551 00681 1

Printed in Great Britain by
Willmer Brothers Limited, Birkenhead
and bound by Tinlings of Liverpool

Contents

Preface

This volume is the second of the *New Light Series*, its companion volume being *New Light On The Gospels*. As with the previous book, this material was first presented in a continuing weekly programme, *Word Of Truth*, broadcast over the international radio station H.C.J.B. in Quito, Ecuador.

Once again acknowledgment is made to the Council and staff of the Australian Institute of Archaeology, of which Institute the author was Director. Without the capable help of Mrs. Helen Strang, Miss Margaret Martin, and Mr. David Searle, this work could not have appeared until a much later time. They have given long hours to this project and I am grateful for their assistance.

C.A.W.

The Australian Institute of Archaeology
174 Collins Street
Melbourne

Introduction

Did you know that priests in ancient Egypt actually put ear-rings in crocodiles? That they fed them with some of the choicest food offered at the temples? Is it news to you that when these creatures died many of them were embalmed just as thoroughly as a noble Egyptian was embalmed? For all this is true, well-attested by the spade of the archaeologist.

Imagine the disgust of native workmen employed by Drs. B. P. Grenfell and A. S. Hunt at the beginning of this century—hoping to find gold, or silver, or at least some other treasure. . . . What did they find? Only embalmed crocodiles! We told the story in our companion volume *New Light On The Gospels*—of how instructions were given to leave the tomb so that excavations could begin elsewhere . . . of how a workman broke the back of one of these sacred creatures and a mass of old papyrus letters poured out.

We are told how the excavators did not immediately recognize the significance of their discovery as to New Testament documents. However, the German scholar Dr. Adolph Deissmann soon revealed to the world that these documents dated to the centuries immediately before, during, and after New Testament times. Not only that, but they were written in the language of everyday people, the speech of the forgotten multitudes who were virtually ignored in the known classical writings of those times. This "everyday" language—*koine* ("common") Greek—was also the language of the New Testament.

In the years that followed further old letters were found in other areas of ancient Egypt and in other countries. The findings were not limited to papyrus—ostraca (broken pottery), parchment, wood, metal, and stone were all used by these people of long ago.

In *New Light On The Gospels* we saw how these records were relevant to the Gospel writings. In this volume we see a similar relevance to the letters of the New Testament. Hence our title, *New Light On New Testament Letters*. We take those letters virtually in the order in which they appear in the Bible, though not in a strict sense. Where two Epistles are touched on, we show that relevance in the one appraisal. Sometimes we go back to the Gospels, for the seed of the teaching developed in the Epistles is invariably found in the Gospels. However, we have been careful not to repeat material used in the companion volume.

To cover all the evidence would be impossible in one small book. Instead, we have selected representative words and subjects in such a way as to touch all the New Testament letters. We find that these documents are indeed the products of New Testament times, and in addition we are delighted to see many points at which the Bible writings become clearer.

In this survey we have not majored on the startling, but on the "everyday". However, in a sense that is also the method of the Holy Spirit of God. For, as we have already seen, the papyrus findings have made it clear that the New Testament was written in *koine* Greek, the language of the man in the street. This dynamic language was ideal for the universal spread of the gospel in the 1st century A.D., and we common people of the 20th century continue to "hear Him gladly" (Mark 12:37).

Prologue: Old Letters And A New Church

(The Acts Of The Apostles)

In this presentation we recognize that the Book of Acts is, in a sense, a bridge between the Gospels and the Epistles. In the Gospels our Lord's teaching is given in His own words. In the Epistles His teaching is developed and becomes the guide for the early Church. But the Acts covers that transitional period of early Church formation, between our Lord's spoken ministry and the written ministry of those whom the Holy Spirit appointed to teach the newly established churches.

In a special sense, then, the Acts is both an epilogue to the Gospels, and a prologue to the Epistles whose setting it so often illustrates. And so, to this "prologue" we briefly turn.

We shall glance at typical words in the Acts of the Apostles—words whose occurrence in ancient papyri and ostraca has given them fresh meaning for us, or has confirmed that those words were in use in New Testament times. Sometimes too we shall find that "everyday" words were brought into the sacred Canon, and given a richer, spiritual significance.

Correct Recording of Geographic Facts

There are also indirect evidences of the background to the Acts—as with one papyrus document which gives details of a tour of inspection about the year A.D. 50. One of the noteworthy points is that Heptanomis is mentioned as a separate district from the Arsinoite district. This was an unknown fact of first century geography, and this particular document is of great interest because it lists various towns that were thriving at that time.

A similar comment can be made about the cities, towns and regions referred to by Luke. It has long been established that Luke's knowledge of detail both as to geography and history is outstanding. Many times it seemed that he had been caught napping, but archaeological evidence has invariably supported him.

Typical of the ways in which the papyrus fragments endorse the geographical background of the Acts is a seemingly insignificant divorce document dating to A.D. 45. This reference is to certain Egyptian districts: the word for "district" is *meris*, and it is so used in Acts 16:12. In days gone by this terminology had been challenged, but the papyrus makes it clear that the New Testament usage was correct.

It is little wonder that Professor Sir William Ramsay, who had earlier discredited Luke as a reputable writer, wrote of him that he is "an historian of the first rank". Luke's knowledge of detail is somewhat paralleled by our Egyptian document already referred to: the point is, each is an authentic document compiled by someone intimately associated with the geography to which he referred.

Well-Known Names
Another "indirect" evidence relates to the frequent use of names well-known in New Testament times. They are not the people referred to in the sacred documents, but it is interesting to see the same names. Thus we read of Taorses, the daughter of Eutychus, a widow who presents a petition to protect the inheritance rights of her sons. Eutychus is a name known in the Acts (chapter 20:9), he being the young man who went to sleep when Paul was teaching. He fell down dead, and was revived by Paul.

We even meet a high official named Theophilus, reminding us of the "Most Excellent Theophilus" of Acts 1:1. In this particular papyrus, dating to about A.D. 1, the title of Theophilus is "politarch", the same title which is known at Acts 17:6. Incidentally, this title was previously unknown in Egyptian papyri and its New Testament usage helped to make the meaning of the word clear.

Another name known in the Acts is Tyrannus, and in a papyrus dating to A.D. 25 Tyrannus receives a letter of commendation from Theon, regarding Theon's brother Heraclides. And there are other common names known in both the Acts of the Apostles and the papyri.

But let us move on to a selection of words from these ancient letters throwing light on the Book of the Acts.

"Ignorant Men"
One interesting word is *idiōtēs*, used at Acts 4:13 after Peter had faithfully proclaimed the good news of salvation before the Jewish rulers. We read at Acts 4:12, 13:

"Neither is there salvation in any other: for there is none other name under heaven given among men, whereby we must be saved. Now when they saw the boldness of Peter and John, and perceived that they were unlearned and ignorant men, they marvelled, and they took knowledge of them, that they had been with Jesus."

The Greek word for "an ignorant man" is *idiōtēs*, and in the papyri this actually refers to a private person in the sense that he is not an official. One papyrus fragment speaks of overseers having been "chosen from magistrates or private persons".

In this verse in Acts we find there is great surprise in the minds of these learned Jewish rulers because these who spoke with such boldness were not learned men as far as priestly training was concerned, neither were they officials of the synagogue, nor were they officers of the Jewish people in any sense. They were private people, fishermen in fact, and yet they had an amazing experience to share with such confidence that the rulers marvelled. It is little wonder we read, "They took knowledge of them, that they had been with Jesus."

Dr. Ruphus Gives An Order

At Acts 7:53 Stephen is giving that great address just before his martyrdom. He refers to the law having been received "by the disposition of angels". The word for *disposition* is *diatagē*, and it is used again at Romans 13:2 where we read, "Whosoever therefore resisteth the power, resisteth the ordinance (*diatagē*) of God: and they that resist shall receive to themselves damnation."

The word occurs in the writings of a physician known as Ruphus of Ephesus, who lived about A.D. 100. He is talking about someone being restored to health after his subsequent way of living is properly ordered. This idea of an ordered way of life is involved in the word *diatagē*. In this case it is the doctor who gives the decree, or order. Some might say that the medical profession is similarly engaged today!

Ruphus himself happened to live and write not far from the time of Luke, who used the same word in the compilation of the Acts of the Apostles. However, the word was not only a medical term. One of the Oxyrhynchus papyri uses it in relation to an order for wine, and another in an order for corn. Further, in an inscription from Lycia, believed to date to the 2nd century A.D., the word is used in connection with divine ordinances, telling us that a certain person will be liable to penalties "appointed by divine ordinances". This is remarkably similar to the passage at Romans 13 where people are expected to submit to the imperial ordinances.

The New Testament word is found in countries extending along the shores of the Mediterranean, and is also used in the Septuagint Version of the Book of Ezra at chapter 4:11. What seemed to be only a New Testament word proves to be a thoroughly accepted word, belonging to the larger world of Bible times.

"I Worship All The Gods"

One document dating to the 2nd or 3rd century B.C. discusses the popular ideas of religion, and is especially critical of the way the gods are feared. It seems that this is a copy of an earlier work, possibly from the philosopher Epicurus or one of his followers. The writer is critical of the attitude of ordinary man, an attitude that is demonstrated by these words: "I fear all the gods and worship them, and to them I wish to make every sacrifice and offering."

This reminds us of the practice at Athens where an altar was built "To The Unknown God" to make sure that no God would be omitted from worship. Of indirect interest also is the fact that the Epicureans were associated with the groups whose forms of worship Paul was denouncing in that place.

The philosophers of Athens objected to Paul's activities, and said that he was a "setter forth" of strange gods. The word used of Paul there is *kataggeleus*, and it means "proclaimer" or "herald". Writers such as H. Cremer insisted that this word was known only in ecclesiastical Greek. However, this seemed to be a strange conclusion because where it is used in the Biblical passage it actually comes from the mouth of a pagan. The problem has now been resolved, for the word was found on a marble stela recording one of the decrees of the Mytilenians, honouring the Emperor Augustus, and dating to about 20 B.C.

The inscription referred to the heralds of the first games to be held. Those heralds had something to shout about—and so did the Apostle Paul with his wonderful new proclamation concerning Jesus and the resurrection. It was not a "strange god" whom Paul was presenting but the only true God. This God did not dwell in temples built by men, for He Himself was the Creator of life. Even the great Athenian Acropolis—to which Paul possibly pointed—could not contain the true God: "God dwelleth not in temples made with hands," he declared (Acts 17:24).

These profound truths were new to many who heard Paul publishing his great message on that hill in Athens —they thought only of "gods" who were visible. So Paul seemed to them as a "babbler"—a word literally meaning a "seed-picker"—a colloquial expression referring to one who picked things out of the gutter.[1]

Unstamped Silver, And Tarsus

One petition dated to A.D. 114 relates to a robbery. Tarmuthis tells how another woman came into her home and picked a quarrel with her, stripping her of her tunic and mantle as well as stealing the money which Tarmuthis had gained by selling vegetables. Later in that same month the woman's husband also came and—"Seizing my lamp, he went up into my house, and stole and carried off a pair of bracelets of *unstamped* silver of the weight of 40 drachmae, my husband being at the time away from home."

This word for *unstamped* is *asēmos*, and it is used in the papyri to refer to someone who is not distinguished from other people by any particular marks. The word is also used in medical language for a disease that has no distinctive symptoms. It is used at Acts 21:39 where the Apostle Paul says, "I am a man which am a Jew of Tarsus, a city of Cilicia, a citizen *of no mean* city: and I beseech thee, suffer me to speak unto the people." Here our word *asēmos*, "unstamped", has been translated "of a mean" or "ordinary". The negative is added, and thus by implication the Apostle Paul is saying that his city is an outstanding city; it is not like unstamped silver (to use the language of the papyri), but it is a tried city, one that has gained the respect of the world.

Gallio in Corinth—Setting A Date

Ever since Adolf Deissmann issued his monumental volume, *Light From The Ancient East* in 1908, further light has been thrown upon the New Testament records. Consider Dr. Deissmann's words: "No tablets have yet been found to enable us to date exactly the years of office of the Procurators Felix and Festus or of the Proconsul Gallio, which would settle any important problems of early Christian history."

An inscription has now been found at Delphi, another city in the province of Achaia, making it possible to set the date of A.D. 51 for the arrival of Gallio in Corinth. The inscription takes the form of a letter from the Emperor Claudius, and it includes a reference to Gallio as "Lucius Junius Gallio, my friend, and the proconsul of Achaia."

"I Will Neither Eat Nor Drink!"

In one letter a young man quoted his mother as having said, "He upsets me—away with him!" and this letter is of interest as regards two different incidents in the New Testament. "Upsets" is the same word used of the Apostle Paul who "turned the world upside down" (Acts 17:6)—he "upset" the world. Secondly, the expression "away with him!" was used by the Jews at the false trial of Jesus Christ—"Away with Him, away with Him, crucify Him!" (John 19:15).

In this same papyrus the young man Theon writes further to his father, "Please do not send for me. I will neither eat nor drink." The relevance of this to the Acts becomes clear when we turn to chapter 23:12, and there we read of Jews who banded themselves together under a curse, declaring they would neither eat nor drink until they had killed Paul.

Another man in the papyrus documents also takes an oath threatening that he will continue to fast until action is taken. We today still hear of such oaths—in India it is fairly common for men to fast so that Government action will be commenced along certain lines. It is not altogether surprising to learn that this modern custom was also known in ancient times, for human nature changes little.

Taking A Surety

We have referred to names used in both the papyri and the Acts. Likewise the name Justus appears in a letter from Alexandria, dating to A.D. 22. We learn that "Justus the sword-bearer is in prison". An amusing point in this letter is the following: "Let me hear about our bald friend, how his hair is growing again on the top . . ."! In this same papyrus the matter of surety in court is referred to, and we are reminded of Jason of whom surety was taken at Acts 17:9, after Paul and his party had preached at Thessalonica, and uproar had followed. The same word for security (*hikanon*) is used in the New Testament and in this papyrus.

Another paprus dating to A.D. 23 is a copy of a form in which a man goes surety for another who has been arrested for debt. Theon, the son of Ammonius, undertakes to produce the prisoner Sarapion within a month, or to pay the amount of the debt.

On Casting Out Demons

At Acts 19:13ff. we read of certain Jews who attempted to use the name of Jesus to perform miracles—to cast out evil spirits. This practice is known in New Testament times, and indeed it has continued on through the centuries.

One papyrus dated to the 3rd century A.D. tells of an invocation put over the head of the one possessed. These are the instructions:

> "Place before him branches of olive, and standing behind him say: Hail spirit of Abraham; hail, spirit of Isaac; hail, spirit of Jacob; *Jesus the Christ*, the holy one, the spirit . . . drive forth the devil from this man, until this unclean demon of Satan shall flee before thee. I adjure thee, O demon, whoever thou art, by the God Sabarbar-bathioth, Sabarbarbathiuth, Sabarbarbathioneth Sabarbar-baphai. Come forth, O demon, whoever thou art, and depart from so and so at once, at once, now. Come forth, O demon, for I chain thee with adamantine chains not to be loosed, and I give you over to black chaos in utter destruction."

An Ancient Lawsuit

A report of a lawsuit, instituted by a man named Pesouris against a nurse Saraeus, for the recovery of a male foundling reminds us of the record in Acts 24 of the prosecution against the Apostle Paul. Here we have a record of the charges and of the events centering around the court case, just as in the case against Paul. The format is similar.

Such documents constantly impress us with the fact

that the records of the New Testament are authentic. Yet our New Testament writings were not preserved on rubbish heaps or in embalmed crocodiles, but were handed down century by century in a way that is unique in all literature, except for the parallel documents of the Old Testament.

It is astonishing that this same gathering and transmission of documents is true in such a special sense of one set of Books that came down through the Jewish people, and of another set that came down through the Christians whom the Jewish leaders opposed so violently. And yet these two sets of Books combine to make one set, and they give a consistent revelation of the one true God, perfectly displayed in the Person of Jesus Christ. Each set of Books has been preserved separately. Each is incomplete without the other; they have been brought together to make one. Those two volumes have become the Bible, one of the greatest heritages of the human race.

And the Acts of the Apostles is an integral part of that heritage.

REFERENCES

[1] *Buried History* 4 (March 1968), p. 5.

1

Writing to Friends At The Capital

(Romans)

There is an old saying, "All roads lead to Rome," and when Paul wrote to the Christians who lived at the capital of the empire, Rome was the centre of attraction for the whole world. It was built on the left bank of the River Tiber and sprawled across seven hills about fifteen miles from the river's mouth. Its narrow winding streets were dirty, and they were flanked by dwellings. More than a million people lived in the city, and half of these were slaves. A high percentage of the others were paupers who lived on a public dole. A very small number of citizens were extremely wealthy.

The Roman historian Seneca refers to the Rome of Biblical days as a "cesspool of iniquity". Writers of ancient history make it abundantly clear that the moral depravity—especially of the nobility—was beyond description. In Romans 1 we read of men who became so depraved that God gave them up. This description fits various cultures of ancient times such as the Canaanites, defeated in the days of Joshua, but it also is true of the Roman civilization itself.

All One In Christ

When Paul wrote to the Christians at this imperial city, he was addressing many different classes—men and women, rich and poor, noblemen and slaves, tent-makers like himself, Jew and Gentile, his bretheren by blood and his new brethren in Christ. All these are included in his closing greetings in chapter 16.

This was a new thing in the world—women gained new status as "sisters" in the Lord; the slave could "break bread" with his master; a new "society" developed whose membership depended solely on faith in Jesus Christ.

Other social unions of the so-called lower classes had by now come into being, for working people had joined into trade unions, not to agitate for better working conditions but to ensure—of all things—a proper burial. In addition, for a few brief hours they enjoyed social life together, able to forget the rigours of their everyday employment. There was little serious thought of "striking", for labourers were too easily replaced.

Life for them was tough. Taxes were a terrible burden, and becoming a Christian did not make their lot in this direction any easier. "Be subject to the higher powers. . . pay your tribute . . . render tribute to whom tribute is due!" Paul wrote to them (Romans 13:1, 6, 7). "Pay your taxes" is the way some modern translators put it.[1]

The Poll Tax

One of the most important taxes was the poll tax,* a flat tax levied on nearly all the population, without regard to income. Some people were exempt, including Romans, citizens of Greek cities, and a limited number of others.

The liability of slaves as regards the poll tax was determined by the liability of their owners,[2] and so even slaves could be placed on the "privileged list". An interesting analogy is that the Christian was once a slave, in bondage, sold to sin, but Christ redeemed him and his name has been added to the most wonderful "privileged list" ever known. But of course the Christian's privilege goes beyond that of a slave fortunate enough to have his name on such a list. The slave remained a slave, but not so the Christian. The Son of God has made him free, and he is free indeed (John 8:36).

*This was instituted in 8 B.C. by Caesar Augustus. See *New Light On The Gospels*, chapter 2, as to its relevance to the birth of Christ.

The poll tax was levied from when a person reached fourteen years of age and it continued until he was sixty. So that nobody could evade this tax the lists were revised by a census every fourteen years. This meant that the longest a person could go without being registered was thirteen years. Even if he was born just after the census took place he would be caught in the next one, fourteen years later. Thus virtually all his income-producing life was covered by the poll tax. The payment of the tax itself was an annual matter.

Taxation In General

In one papyrus document there are at least four different taxes referred to as payable at the one time. These were the poll tax, levied on all but the privileged classes. Secondly, there was a tax on particular trades, in this case the weaving trade. Thirdly, there was a tax on pigs, and fourthly there was an assessment for the maintenance of embankments. The tax on an embankment was sometimes paid by labour instead of by cash. One papyrus implies that five days' personal work was the alternative to the payment of this tax in cash.

At least fifteen different taxes were imposed on the Egyptians in the Roman period. Imports, exports, land, produce, trades, animals—they were all taxed. Even the mortgage of land involved taxation, and the accession of the emperor was also an occasion for a special tax. The tax burden was heavy indeed.

From other papyrus documents we find that people often ran away, simply because they could not pay all the taxes. We even find references to villages being virtually deserted as a result of these heavy impositions on the people, for thousands fled to the cities where they could be lost in the crowds. This probably explains why poll declarations someties mention that no alien or person from outside the city is living under the same roof at the time of the census.

And so, when Paul urged those Christians at Rome, "Pay your taxes!" it was no light thing he was asking. Little wonder that for many years Christians were not thought to be a potential threat to the well-being of the empire. Followers of Christ became better citizens of Rome.

Submitting To Roman Emperors

But, as we saw, Paul did not only write, "Pay your taxes": he went considerably further. To those Christians, many of them suffering indignity and distress, he wrote, "Be subject to the higher powers" (Romans 13:1).

Those who live in democratic countries do not immediately recognize the implications of injunctions such as this. At times we might be discontented with a particular government, but in the main Western countries know great liberty. Democracy offers freedom and relative equality such as many living under other forms of government long for. But these Christians in Rome did not live under a democratic government. They lived under Roman emperors some of whom were ruthless tyrants. The historian Suetonius, who lived from A.D. 75 to A.D. 160, writes of the punishments that were inflicted on the Christians—"a set of men adhering to a novel and mischievous superstition."

Pliny the Younger (A.D. 62–113) writes to the Emperor Trajan as to his treatment of Christians:

> "Meanwhile, this is the course that I have adopted in the case of those brought before me as Christians. I ask them if they are Christians. If they admit it I repeat the question a second and a third time, threatening capital punishment; if they persist I sentence them to death. For I do not doubt that, whatever kind of crime it may be to which they have confessed, their pertinacity and inflexible obstinacy should certainly be punished."[3]

Christians Burned As Living Torches

Other writers make it clear that to embrace Christianity was to risk death. Tacitus writes that Christians were deliberately and falsely blamed for the great fire of Rome in A.D. 64. He tells of a rumour that Nero had actually ordered this fire to be lit. We quote:

"And so, to get rid of this rumour, Nero set up as the culprits and punished with the utmost refinement of cruelty a class hated for their abominations, who are commonly called Christians. Christus, from whom their name is derived, was executed at the hands of the procurator Pontius Pilate in the reign of Tiberius. Checked for the moment, this pernicious superstition again broke out, not only in Judaea, the source of the evil, but even in Rome, that receptacle for everything that is sordid and degrading from every quarter of the globe, which there finds a following. Accordingly, arrest was first made of those who confessed; then, on their evidence, an immense multitude was convicted, not so much on the charge of arson as because of hatred of the human race. Besides being put to death they were made to serve as objects of amusement; they were clad in the hides of beasts and torn to death by dogs; others were crucified, others set on fire to serve to illuminate the night when daylight failed. Nero had thrown open his grounds for the display, and was putting on a show in the circus, where he mingled with the people in the dress of a charioteer or drove about in his chariot. All this gave rise to a feeling of pity, even towards men whose guilt merited the most exemplary punishment; for it was felt that they were being destroyed not for the public good but to gratify the cruelty of an individual."[4]

This took place after Paul had written to the Christians at Rome, but undoubtedly the Romans as such had no love for the Christians. At best they tolerated what to them seemed atheistic teachings—for the Romans could not understand why the Christians rejected all gods but their own, and would allow no images, not even of their own God.

Was Paul's Advice Foolish?
At first sight it might seem that Paul's advice was wrong. How foolish, humanly speaking, to submit to these men who at times were so opposed to the revelation of God! But Christianity *was* "foolishness" in the eyes of men,

and the very Founder of Christianity died on a Roman cross. Paul himself was eventually to go to Rome, there to meet his death at the orders of the Emperor himself. He was prepared to "practise what he preached" no matter what the cost. As he himself said in this very letter to the Romans, "For I reckon that the sufferings of this present time are not worthy to be compared with the glory which shall be revealed in us" (Romans 8:18).

So he wrote to the Roman Christians, "Submit to the higher powers." One aspect of this paradoxical teaching is that heavenly values do not necessarily correspond to those of earth. The worst the Romans could do was to destroy a man's earthly life, but the Christian's life was eternal, going beyond earthly ties.

The Hope For "Righteous Judgment"

Paul knew that righteous judgment belonged to God, even if not to a Roman Caesar, and the Christian's hope was therefore sure. The Apostle actually uses this term "righteous judgment" (at Romans 2:5) as he writes to these Christians. He uses the word *dikaiokrisia* which was supposed to be used only in ecclesiastical writings. Now it has been found in an inscription dating to A.D. 303. A former priest named Aurelius Demetrius Nilus had a petition written to the Prefect of Egypt and stated he was hoping that "righteous judgment" would be delivered because of the character of the Prefect to whom the petition was addressed.

Interestingly enough, in this petition the point is made that someone else is writing for him because he himself cannot write. The man was pleading for a just sentence, and clearly the scribe used this word because it was common in official usage. The word is found to have another meaning of "equal" or "well-balanced" as in the case of an evenly-running chariot. So it came to mean fair, lawful or just.[5]

This then is the term used at Romans 2:5: "But after thy hardness and impenitent heart treasurest up unto thyself wrath against the day of wrath and revelation of the *righteous judgment* of God." Paul used it again at

II Thessalonians 1:5—"Which is a manifest token of the *righteous judgment* of God, that ye may be counted worthy of the kingdom of God, for which ye also suffer;" and the Lord Jesus Christ used it at John 7:24: "Judge not according to the appearance, but judge *righteous judgment*."

It was not only a Biblical word after all, but the New Testament writers perfectly understood this term from their own background.

The Holy Spirit Takes An Interest In Our Infirmities
Paul knew the problems and sufferings of these people. Had not he himself suffered so constantly? In His wisdom the Holy Spirit had chosen one ideally equipped to encourage the disciples, and Paul on *his* part knew by experience that the Holy Spirit also sympathizes in our distresses. To explain this Paul wrote at Romans 8:26, "Likewise the Spirit also *helpeth* our infirmities: for we know not what we should pray for as we ought: but the Spirit Himself maketh intercession for us, with groanings which cannot be uttered."

The word translated "helpeth" is *sunantilambanomai*, meaning literally "lends a hand along with," "takes a share in," or "takes an interest in," and it occurs also at Luke 10:40: Martha was involved in "much serving," and she went to the Lord and said, "Do you not care that my sister has left me to serve alone?" Martha went on to say, "Tell her therefore that she may *help* me"— and she used this same word. Martha was saying, "Tell her to *take her share*." "Tell her to *take an interest in* my side of the work."

The word has been found in various inscriptions. In the Temple of Apollo at Delphi it relates to *helping* with things profitable for the city, this being an inscription written 270 years before Christ. A similar inscription was found at Pergamum, dating to about 250 B.C.

It occurs again in a papyrus letter from El-Hibeh in Egypt, dating to about 238 B.C., and it includes the expression, "Thou wilt therefore do well *to take part* zealously in the things relating thereto."

The Paraclete
Applying this new knowledge to Romans 8:26, then, we learn that the Holy Spirit of God *takes an interest* in our need—He comes alongside to help. Thus we have a noteworthy association with another word used elsewhere to tell us about the Holy Spirit. We refer to the word *paraklētos*, which is applied in various ways—"advocate", "representative at a trial," "intercessor," "one who strengthens." It is well-attested in many papyrus documents, especially with the meaning of "advocate"–the accused's friend—in court cases.

The word is used of our Lord Himself at I John 2:1, and of the Holy Spirit at John 14:16, 26; 15:26; and 16:7.* The Holy Spirit, the Comforter, has come, and He stands alongside us in our need. But that is not all, for we are told at I John 2:1 that Christ Himself is our Advocate, our Paraclete. He and the Holy Spirit of God are in complete agreement in Their interest on our behalf. The Holy Spirit is "Another Comforter"—One of the same nature as the One speaking, the One Who is Himself a "Comforter". The Holy Spirit makes intercession for us with groanings that cannot be uttered (Romans 8:26), and Christ Himself is also our Advocate with the Father (I John 2:1).

Thus we see how our two words—*sunantilambanomai* and *paraklētos*—come together. The Holy Spirit *helps* our infirmities (Romans 8:26); He is our Advocate, and likewise Christ Himself is our Advocate.

At Romans 8:26, then, the Apostle was using a word well-known in the local background, and ennobling it, giving it a spiritual significance which must have been a real comfort to those who received his letter.

Quartus—A Brother: And New Relationships
Another example of a word being employed to convey a deeper truth than in its original usage is *adelphos*. This word means "brother" in Greek, and it came also to mean members of the community who were not

*Further discussed in *New Light On The Gospels*, chapter 11.

necessarily related by blood. This is illustrated by a papyrus letter dated to A.D. 1 where Didymus writes concerning "Ammonio, the brother".[6] At various places in the papyri we find this word *adelphos*, "*the brother*," associated with the fraternity and not necessarily referring to blood relationship.

In the New Testament it came to mean "members of Christ's new family", blood brothers in the sense that they were bought by His blood.

That is the meaning we find in such references as Romans 16:23, ". . . Erastus the chamberlain of the city saluteth you, and Quartus *a brother*". A similar usage is at II Peter 3:15, ". . . even as our beloved *brother* Paul." We read also at Philippians 1:14 of those who are "*brethren* in the Lord". This goes beyond human relationships, whether of blood, race, or institution.

We referred to "Quartus a brother"; we know no more about him, but we know enough. He was a brother in Christ—he had entered into a new relationship with other believers, his "brothers in Christ".

In that same chapter we see how this relationship extended to women also as they became partners in the service of God. So the Apostle wrote to commend a woman named Phoebe who was apparently visiting Rome. He writes, "I commend unto you Phoebe our sister, which is a servant of the church which is at Cenchrea : that you receive her in the Lord, as becometh saints . . ." Romans 16:1).

In another connection this can also be linked with yet another comment of Paul at II Corinthians 3:3. Some professing Christians had challenged his apostolic authority. "Do we—as some others do—need letters of commendation *to* you? Or do we need letters of commendation *from* you?" he asks.

In both these letters he touched on the matter of commendation, and he was referring to a practice of his times—the sending of a letter of commendation as to the credentials of one visiting a new area, or being introduced to other people.

A very good example of a letter of commendation, dating to approximately A.D. 25, reads as follows:

"Theon to his esteemed Tyrannus, many greetings. Heraclides, the bearer of this letter, is my brother. I therefore entreat you with all my power to treat him as your protégé. I have also written to your brother Hermias asking him to communicate with you about him. You will confer upon me a very great favour if Heraclides gains your notice. Before all else you have my good wishes for unbroken health and prosperity. Good-bye."[7]

Not many churches today bother about "letters of commendation"—often a telephone call has the same practical effect. But even today there is sometimes good reason for such a guarantee against those who would advance false claims to gain Christian privileges.

As well as being a necessary safeguard, letters of commendation pointed to the closeness of fellowship among early Christians. That oneness in Christ was also shown in various letters which demonstrate that Christians cared for each other. They were members of one family, and felt for each other in their special needs.

Helping A Brother Whose Children Were Sold
To illustrate this here is a letter written on behalf of a Christian named Pamonthius. He had fallen into debt and his children had been seized. He himself had been arrested, but was set free on bail, and now there is an appeal for help from other Christian friends:

"To those who have fallen into misfortune the word of God exhorts us to give succour; to all, and most to our brethren. Our brother Pamonthius, having fallen into no common vicissitudes, has suffered most shamefully at the hands of pitiless and godless men. As a result he is compelled, one might almost say, to lose our blessed hope. For this reason he besought us to make application by these present letters to your brotherliness, setting forth all his affairs, to the end that you too, knowing thereof, may help him, remembering the command of the blessed

29

Apostle not to neglect those who are weak, not only in the Faith but even in the affairs of this world."[8]

In conclusion there is a request that Pamonthius be helped speedily, for his children have been carried off into slavery. The letter points to the true brotherly love and concern in the hearts of these early Christian people.

In the next letter[9] of this particular series, dating to the same time, the story is continued. Those who are writing make it clear that they have great sympathy for their brother Pamonthius, a former wine-seller. The brethren are urged to show love and compassion in collecting funds from the Christians. Once again, the language they use in this papyrus document is illustrative of so much in the New Testament: "Whatever we could find we have given him; yea, we have done even beyond our means." We are reminded of the Philippians who gave beyond their means for the cause of their brother Paul who was even then imprisoned.

On Breaking Down Barriers

Then again, as we read of the urgent request that a collection be taken for this man Pamonthius, we are reminded of the collection for the needy saints of Jerusalem (Romans 15:25–27). In passing, as we read of the funds to be placed under seal so that they could not be tampered with, we recall that Christians too are sealed by the Holy Spirit of God—no power can break *that* seal.

The spirit of these early Christians is very similar to that of Paul as he tells how Christians of Macedonia and Achaia have collected funds for the believers in Jerusalem. The word Paul uses for "collection" is the Greek word *koinōnia* and one particular papyrus[10] dating to approximately A.D. 210 refers to the different methods of sheltering robbers, in which "some do so because they are *partners* in their misdeeds, others without sharing in these . . ."

As we read of these "partners" we have the same word that Paul uses as to those entering into partnership

30

for the relief of needy saints in Jerusalem. The word implies active participation, and the result depends on the co-operation of the receiver as well as the action of the giver. Thus these proud Jewish Christians at Jerusalem had to be prepared to receive, and the Gentiles on their part had to give sacrificially. This was partnership, sharing. This is a striking example of how the Christian gospel had broken down barriers between Jew and Gentile.

And as we think of barriers being broken down it is wonderful to see this same word used at such places as II Corinthians 13:14—"the *koinōnia*, the fellowship, of the Holy Spirit be with you all." Instead of separation, there is a giving and a receiving between the Christian and the Holy Spirit of God Himself.

The Collection For The Saints

We have just seen that when Paul wrote in Romans 15 about that collection for the saints in Jerusalem he used the word *koinōnia*, which has the idea of sharing, having things in common. When he wrote about it to the Christians at Corinth he used another word, for at I Corinthians 16:1, 2 we find the Greek word *logia*.

In earlier times it was common to suggest that this word was invented by Paul. However, derivations of it have now been found on papyrus and ostraca in Egypt and other places. It often relates to collections for religious purposes associated with a god or a temple, and against this background it is interesting to see how Paul employs it concerning a collection of money to be used for poor Christians.

One ostracon dates to 4 August A.D. 63, and comes from Thebes in Egypt. In this a man by the name of Psenamunis acknowledges receipt of certain funds, "being the *collection* of Isis on behalf of the public works." Another inscription dating to the 1st century A.D. at Smyrna lists various religious gifts, including several *objects* for the "*collection* and procession of the gods," and again the word for "collection" is that which Paul used.

31

REFERENCES

[1] E.g. in *Living Letters*, translated by Kenneth N. Taylor.
[2] Pap. No. 714, dating to A.D. 122.
[3] Bettenson, H. (Ed.) *Documents Of The Christian Church*, p. 4.
[4] *Ibid.*, p. 1.
[5] Furness, J. M. *Vital Words Of The Bible*, p. 76.
[6] Oxy. Pap. No. 79.
[7] Oxy. Pap. No. 292.
[8] Pap. No. 1915.
[9] Pap. No. 1916.
[10] Oxy. Pap. No. XII 1408.

2

Cleansing For Castaways At Corinth

(I and II Corinthians)

Paul wrote two letters to the Christians at Corinth (I and II Corinthians) during his third missionary journey (Acts 18:23—21:20). It is widely accepted that the first letter was written in the spring of A.D. 57, while the second is dated to the autumn of the same year.

Corinth, situated on an isthmus between the Ionian and Aegean Seas, was the largest and most famous city of all Greece. It was an important military and commercial centre, and was in an ideal location as a trade link between the East and the West. Trade brought rapid growth in wealth, which produced a culture which sought luxury and a somewhat "second-hand" form of philosophy and speculation. Corinth could not boast of one native scholar and writer of fame.

The prevailing attitude was that people came to Corinth to have a good time. Although it was famous for its commercial wealth, Corinth was notorious for its moral degradation. The saying "To live as the Corinthians do" was synonymous with living a profligate life. Mystery religions found fertile soil in Corinth. The worship of the goddess Aphrodite was associated with the utmost licentiousness, and her one thousand priestesses were little more than religious prostitutes.

In the last chapter we saw that Romans 1 was an accurate description of the moral climate at Rome, but it is equally true that that passage, written from Corinth, gives a vivid picture of the corruption prevalent there.

When Paul left Corinth he paid a visit to Jerusalem

33

and then went to Ephesus. There he heard distressing news as to the Corinthian Church from the household of Chloe. Though surrounded by debauchery, the Church at Corinth had grown, but we find significant glimpses of depravity. False preachers had crept in, and under the pretext of Christian liberty they urged a licentious way of life—divisions and moral lapses followed, and there were serious departures from Christian standards of faith, purity, and love.

Against this background we read of Paul guarding against being a "castaway". As our special topic from these two Corinthian Epistles we have taken a concept from his statement at I Corinthians 9:27: "But I keep under my body, and bring it into subjection: lest that by any means, when I have preached to others, I myself should be a *castaway*." This is especially relevant to the background of Corinthians, for if ever Christians were to be "castaway" by God, we would expect such a judgment on those Corinthians.

Worthless Castaways And Imperishable Words

To understand this term we consider an archaeological point. We quote from Dr. Adolf Deissmann: "On worthless castaway potsherds a poor man writes the imperishable words that are the heritage of the poor." Potsherds were broken pieces of pottery—sometimes known simply as "sherds", or "ostraca". Poorer people who could not afford other writing materials actually wrote on these pottery fragments.

Ostraca have been popular for writing from the 6th century B.C., and they were used extensively throughout the ancient Mediterranean world. Many different languages have been utilised on these ancient "scrap" records, but writing in the Greek script is the most common. It ranges over a thousand years of history, with the New Testament period well covered by these discarded voices from the past. These writings on earthenware fragments deal with similar subjects to those inscribed on papyrus, including many facets of everyday life, but their texts are shorter because of their size—the majority of the

34

texts inscribed on potsherds are in fact tax receipts.

We said that the potsherd was a writing medium for the poorer classes, being the cheapest writing material available—it was simply a matter of going along to the nearest rubbish heap and selecting one's own "paper" on which to write. Ostraca were there for the taking.

Broken Earthenware—Worthless?

The question might well be asked. "Why was not the importance of writings on broken pieces of pottery recognized before this century?" Dr. Deissmann has an interesting comment on this:

> "I am reminded of a sentence in one of Pastor von Bodelschwingh's annual reports of a scrap-collecting organization for the support of the Bethel charities near Bielefeld. 'Nothing is absolutely worthless,' he says, 'except bits of broken earthenware and the fag-ends of cigars,' and the opinion seems to have been shared by the peasants of Egypt, at least so far as bits of pottery were concerned. They rummaged among ancient ruins, and whenever they came across such pitiable objects as bits of earthenware vessels, they threw them away at once. Many a European with a scholar's training must have been quite convinced that ancient potsherds were valueless, even when there was writing visible on them; otherwise one cannot understand why they were to all intents and purposes ignored by research for so long a time, comparatively. After all, what can there be more pitiful than an earthen potsherd? The prophet in his emphatic irony could think of no image more apt to describe man's nothingness than that of a potsherd among potsherds: 'Woe unto him that striveth with his Maker! A potsherd among the potsherds of the earth!' (Isaiah 45:9)"[1]

Bible Verses On Potsherds

Of great interest to the Bible student is the fact that the writings on many of these potsherds are Bible verses, and it becomes clear that the gospel was in the hands of everyday people. Even the Christian who was poverty-

35

stricken in Egypt could have part of the Word of God written down.

We saw that Dr. Deissmann referred to these seemingly worthless pieces as "castaway" potsherds. The vessel had been broken and so the fragments were "castaway"—no longer of any use. But those rejected scraps, of little value now for their original purpose, are to become valuable because on one a receipt will be written, or even a private letter. And for many a Christian a precious portion of the Word of God will be inscribed on that castaway ostracon.

The word "castaway" which Paul uses at I Corinthians 9:27 is actually *adokimos*, and it means literally "unapproved" or "rejected". A water pot which had been cracked was no longer useful for its original purpose as a water container, so it was *adokimos*—a castaway–put on the shelf. The spiritual parallel, against which Paul is warning, is that a man can lose his privileged place of service. He is then relegated to some secondary service, like the cracked pot that was put on one side. That broken vessel is no longer of value for containing water, but it is still possibly useful for some minor purpose such as holding household objects.

This new light is interesting, if only to show that the Apostle Paul was not suggesting that one who was rejected from his special calling thereby lost his salvation. Paul would teach us that a man could become ineffective so far as his primary service was concerned and become *adokimos*—a castaway—able to do only secondary service as compared to the great work with which God would have entrusted him. The verse is specifically relevant to service as such, and not to salvation.

This word *adokimos* is used at other places in the Epistles,* always in the sense of rejection, "castaway".

Cleansing The Castaway
Paul shows the practical application of this concept as

*Romans 1:28; II Corinthians 13:5–7; II Timothy 3:8; Titus 1:16; Hebrews 6:8.

36

he adds a word of advice for the Corinthians regarding one man who had surely become "castaway", "unapproved." That man, guilty of a great moral lapse, had repented, and the Christians are urged to forgive him, "lest perhaps such a one should be swallowed up with overmuch sorrow" (II Corinthians 2:7).

The Apostle goes on in the next verse to urge them to confirm their love towards the one who had so grievously failed. God could cleanse and renew the castaway—and the church should show *their* love in the spirit of Christ.

The Apostle Paul used yet another word associated with pottery, as he told how some men had looked on him "as the *filth* of the world (I Corinthians 4:13). The word is *perikatharma*. This is "a term of the deepest opprobrium, drawn from the 'rinsing' of a dirty vessel". The term derives from the "most wretched and outcast" of vessels. In the same verse Paul says that some men regarded him as the "off-scouring of all things". This word referred to the scrapings from a dirty vessel. This Pharisee of the Pharisees was prepared to have no reputation at all, if necessary, as he took his place alongside the Christ Whom men had crucified.

Put In Trust With The Gospel

The positive form of the word *adokimos* is *dokimos*, the "a" denoting the negative. One of the places where a derivative of it is used is I Thessalonians 2:4: "As we were allowed of God to be put in trust with the gospel, even so we speak." That is how it is in the Authorized Version, but actually it should be: "... we have been approved of God ..."

In the papyri we read of a marriage contract dating to 311 B.C.[2] One of the conditions is that in the event of the husband failing in his duty, witnesses would be appointed of whom both the husband and the wife *approved*. In the contract the parties could separate, in the event of failure, and the dowry was to be returned. God in His grace has *approved* of us failing mortals, even putting us in trust with His gospel. We are approved of God, we hear His voice, and speak as His messengers.

The word is also used in another sense, for at James 1:13 and at I Peter 1:7 this word *dokimos* is used concerning the *proving* of one's faith.

Faith—Tested In A Crucible

The word appears in the papyri where coins are being tested to see whether they are genuine or false. Against this background the statement at I Peter 1:7 is better understood. There Peter says:

"That the *trial* of your faith, being much more precious than of gold that perisheth, though it be tried with fire, might be found unto praise and honour and glory at the appearing of Jesus Christ."

Here it is as though faith is being put in a crucible and tested to prove whether it is true or false, real or counterfeit, and when it is found to be the real thing it is far more precious than gold tried by fire. The practical application is that we should recognize that we are being tested as gold in the fire, and we should aim always to live to the praise, honour, and glory of Him Whom having not seen we love—as Peter reminds us in the next verse.

The Christians to whom Paul wrote at Corinth knew this testing in their own experience—they had to decide on very practical issues: such as whether they would eat at the table of the Lord—or at the table of demons (I Corinthians 10:21). There are papyrus fragments that refer to the practice of eating at the table of heathen gods.

Dining At Our Lord's Table

One fragment told of a man who had the privilege of "dining at the table of the lord Serapis", and the invitation was for 3 o'clock in the afternoon.[8] Though this function was actually in a private house, it was designated as being "at the table of Serapis", one of the widely worshipped gods of the Egyptian people.

In ancient times this concept of dining at a table was not always limited to a social relationship, but could also involve active identification with the god concerned —as with Serapis in the fragment we are considering.

We who are Christians have the honour of dining, not at the table of false gods or demons, but at the table of the Son of God Himself. We are "seated together in heavenly places in Christ Jesus" (Ephesians 2:6).

Another point from this fragment is that the invitation is to a meal commencing at 3 o'clock in the afternoon. In our Lord's parable of the great supper the guests were invited in the daylight hours, as is shown by the fact that some did not come but got on with the day's work. The feasting obviously went on for many hours, for the man without the wedding garment was thrown out into the darkness—night had long since fallen.

On Cutting A Woman's Hair
We have seen that Paul is taking practical points on which the Corinthians need guidance. He explains spiritual principles against the local situation.

Another reminder that these New Testament letters are set against the background of their times comes from a fragment dating to the reign of the Roman Emperor Vespasian, at the end of the 1st century A.D.[4] It is a substantial portion of a well-known play concerning a churlish soldier named Polemo who has so mistreated his beloved Glycera that she eventually leaves him.

The reason for his abusing her is his jealousy. Then, in a fit of violence, he went so far as to cut off her hair. Little wonder that Glycera deserted him! She came from an honourable family, and was utterly shamed by this dastardly act. But Polemo hears from his slave Doris that there is a possibility of Glycera's forgiveness, and he is so elated that he promises Doris her freedom. Reconciliation takes place, and Glycera's father urges Polemo never to commit such a reckless deed again.

This reminder of the importance of long hair to a woman in New Testament times is pertinent to I Corinthians 11:6: "It is a shame for a woman to be shorn or shaven." A woman whose hair was "shaven" could be mistaken for a prostitute.

39

And Paul does not only speak about a *woman's* hair —he also has a comment about men whose hair is too long! This is what we read at I Corinthians 11:14: "Doth not even nature itself teach you, that, if a man have long hair, it is a shame unto him?"

In this connection it is worth noting that in the early Church short hair was regarded as the mark of the orthodox Christian teacher, as compared with the flowing locks of the heathen philosopher. So Christian men were not to allow their hair to grow as long as a woman's.

The problem was not limited to *Christian* teachers, for one papyrus document from Egypt is actually a complaint against a priest who is charged with letting his hair grow too long.[5]

The Dead Sea Scrolls And
The "Angels Who Accompany The Troops"

The Dead Sea Scrolls have illuminated another subject touched on in this same chapter which deals with a woman's hair. Paul speaks of veiling in the context of a woman's subjection, and at verse 10 of the chapter we find the difficult clause, "For this cause ought the woman to have power on her head because of the angels." What is meant by this expression, "because of the angels?" In the Dead Sea Scroll known as the "War of the Sons of Light and the Sons of Darkness" we learn that the soldiers engaged against the forces of evil are to keep themselves pure "because of the angels who accompany the troops". The angels could not help these human forces if they were offended by impurity.

Anathema—Cursed!

Another word on which the papyrus throws light is at I Corinthians 16:22 where we read: "If any man love not the Lord Jesus Christ let him be *anathema maran-atha*" —*anathema* being the literal Greek word for "a curse". Once again it was supposed to be only a Bible word, but it also turns up in a collection of cursing tablets dating to the 1st and 2nd centuries A.D. At the end of one particular series of curses there is a whole line taken up for the word *anathema*, spelt out in large letters—clearly it is a concluding "curse". In the body of the text itself three times it is stated "we curse them". Thus, again a so-called Biblical word is found in secular writings.

A Thorn In The Flesh

One letter dating to the 3rd century A.D.[6] tells of a mother's anxiety for her son who has injured his foot. The letter is actually in very bad Greek, but it clearly demonstrates the worrying love of a mother for her boy.

A friend had told her that her son "had a sore foot owing to a splinter. And I was troubled because you were only able to walk so slowly". It goes on to say that her friend told her that there was nothing much the matter with the boy. An interesting point about this letter is that it not only shows the anxiety of a mother, but that the word *skolops* is used for "splinter"—though spelled badly by her! This is one of the evidences now available to show that this word which originally meant "stake" had come to mean "splinter" or "thorn", and this is just how the Apostle Paul uses it at II Corinthians 12:7 where he tells us that there was given to him a "thorn"—a *skolops*—in the flesh. He used the same word that this mother used about the splinter in her boy's foot.

From another papyrus we learn that a man fell from a tree and a splinter penetrated his eye, causing him blindness after some time. In one of the so-called "magical papyri" the sorcerer says of the loved one: "If she wants to lie down, strew beneath her prickly branches, and thorns upon her temples,"[7] and here "thorns" is a plural form of this same word *skolops*.

Many conjectures have been made as to the irritant—the *skolops*—in the life of Paul. Perhaps it is best that we do not know its actual nature, for as a result we are encouraged to endure if and when *we* have some persistent thorn in the flesh. We too, like Paul, can know the Lord's voice saying, "My grace is sufficient for thee:

41

for My strength is made perfect in weakness" (II Corinthians 12:9).

Perhaps it was especially appropriate to make such a statement to these particular believers, living as they did against the exceedingly difficult background of pagan Corinth.

Did Paul Know Christ In The Flesh?

Our expression "thorn in the flesh" reminds us of another occasion on which Paul used this word "flesh" (*sarx*). Dr. J. H. Moulton refers to an argument put forward by the German theologian, Johannes Weiss, in his book *Paul and Jesus*. In this Johannes Weiss suggests that the text "Even if we have known Christ in the flesh, yet now we know Him so no more" (II Corinthians 5:16) "necessarily implies that Paul really had seen Jesus".[8] Paul, as Saul of Tarsus, was in Jerusalem before the Passion, and studied under the famous Gamaliel. The Acts of the Apostles show that he was in Jerusalem soon after the crucifixion.

Dr. Moulton refers to Paul's statement in I Corinthians 7 on divorce, and suggests that very possibly Saul of Tarsus was one of the deputation sent to question our Lord on this matter (Matthew 19:1ff.). Saul was a "Hebrew of the Hebrews, as touching the law, a Pharisee" (Philippians 3:5), and it would not be unlikely that such a brilliant man would be in that deputation. The point is interesting, though purely conjectural.

Apion, Like Paul, Saved From "Peril In The Sea"

Another letter, from Apion (an Egyptian soldier in the Roman army) to his father Epimachus, dates to the 2nd century A.D. In it Apion refers to the fact that he has been saved from "*peril in the sea*," using the same root words by which the Apostle Paul described a similar experience (referred to at II Corinthians 11:26). Actually Paul used better Greek constructions.

In a letter to his sister Sabina, Apion sends greetings to various friends. Capito he greets "much", just as Paul says to the Corinthian Christians that Aquila and Priscilla greeted them "much in the Lord" (I Corinthians 16:19). Our Egyptian soldier greets several other friends, and we are reminded of the style of some New Testament letters where the writer sent greetings to various persons. This is common practice in papyrus letters, and it is also seen frequently in the letters of Paul.

Taking A Roman Name

In this letter we find too that our friend Apion has taken a new name. "Moreover," he tells his father, "My name is Antonis Maximus"—and we touch on a custom which is seen several times in the New Testament. Apion, the Egyptian, is engaged in the Roman army, and so he is honoured with a Roman name.

When Saul of Tarsus went into Gentile country to preach the gospel he also assumed his Roman name— Saul of Tarsus was Paul, the Apostle to the Gentiles. "Then Saul (who also is called Paul), filled with the Holy Ghost, set his eyes on him" we read at Acts 13:9. Another example is that Silas is known also as Silvanus (Acts 15:32–40).

In the case of our Egyptian soldier there was a measure of pride in this assumption of a new name, and the letter indicates his desire to do well in his present occupation. "Thou hast taught me well, and I therefore hope to advance quickly," he writes to his father. Unlike Apion, Paul did not hope to advance through the lawful assumption of a Roman name: he was not advancing himself, but he *was* advancing the cause of the gospel —that he might by all means save some (I Corinthians 9:22).

REFERENCES

[1]Deissmann, A. *Light From The Ancient East*, pp. 42f.
[2]Milligan G. *Selections From The Greek Papyri*, p. 1.
[3]Oxy. Pap. No. 523, 2nd century A.D.
[4]Oxy. Pap. No. 211.
[5]Milligan G. *Ibid.*, p. 83, B.G.U. 16, A.D. 159f.

[6]*Ibid.*, pp. 104f., B.G.U. 380, 3rd century A.D.

[7]Moulton, J. H. and Milligan, G. *The Vocabulary Of The Greek Testament*, p. 579.

[8]Moulton, J. H. *From Egyptian Rubbish-Heaps*, pp. 72ff.

3

Setting Slaves Free

(*Galatians*)

The Background

We come to Paul's Epistle to the Galatians. On his first missionary journey he visited south Galatia, and possibly north Galatia as well. Acts 16:6 is taken by some scholars as an indication that on his second missionary journey Paul was going through all the region of Galatia as he delivered the ordinances which the Christians were to observe. The argument is that on this second tour he was visiting various churches already established.

Paul again visited the Galatian Christians on his third missionary journey, as shown by Acts 18:23. Acts 19 makes it clear that he went on to Ephesus, and a long absence from his Galatian friends followed. In that absence Judaizing teachers came into Galatia and they violently opposed Paul and his teaching. Because he could not return to Galatia immediately, he wrote this Epistle (Galatians 4:19ff.).

By their own national history the Galatians were known as a fickle people, and that is shown also in their attitude to Paul. First they were ready to receive him as an angel, even to the "plucking out of their own eyes" to help him (Galatians 4:15), but they were soon moved by false teachers to accept "another gospel". All too soon they were ready to "bite and devour one another".

Paul set out to refute the Judaizers, to insist on his own Apostleship, and to give a clear statement of the doctrine of justification by faith. He sternly rebuked the Galatians for the extent to which they had reverted to spiritual bondage—they had forsaken their new liberty in Christ. Galatians assures us that the Christian is set free from the bondage of the law, for Christ has fully paid sin's penalty.

Christ Was "Placarded"

At chapter 3:1 the Galatians are reminded that Jesus Christ had been "evidently set forth, crucified among you". That was how He paid the price. This word for "set forth" (*prographō*) is known in various papyrus records—one good example centering around a very human reference, in an incident that could be multiplied through many ages and cultures. A father declares that he will no longer be responsible for his son's debts because he had squandered so much in "riotous living". But the man considered that it was not enough to make this declaration orally, so he had a notice "posted up" —it was in the form of a public placard to ensure that all could know.

By Paul's use of the word *prographō* in Galatians he is reminding us that the crucifixion of Christ was not carried out in secret. Though He is the very Son of God, He allowed Himself to be publicly displayed on a cross as though He were a criminal. He was "placarded" before the world. As a result, the world could see that our debt is paid, the full price of our redemption has been met.

But many of these Galatian Christians did not recognize the great privilege, which was theirs, and were all too ready to revert to elements of the spiritual bondage from which they had been released by Christ's death.

1st Century Slaves

To understand what Paul is saying to the Galatians about their new freedom we need to know something of the conditions of slaves and the benefits of redemption in the 1st century A.D.

The whole concept of slavery was of special significance for early Christians. We saw that half the population of Rome were slaves—this does not mean they were inferior types, for they were sometimes highly educated men of advanced culture. Some intelligent, well-educated slaves were the tutors of their master's children.

Selling Slaves At Auction

The conditions of slaves was at times terribly sad, and one wonders how even some of the practical problems were resolved—as with one papyrus dating to A.D. 186[1] which tells about the auction of a slave. Three young men—themselves under age—owned two-thirds of a male slave. The other third was owned by the half-brother of the three young men, and now the slave was to be auctioned so that the three brothers could sell their two-thirds' interest. The slave's name was Sarapion, and he was aged about thirty. The document tells us that at the public auction two-thirds of the slave would be handed over to the highest bidder.

We even find that there were *stigmata*—or brands—on the wrists of some slaves.[2] In this way they could be easily identified if they ran away, and it was the proof of ownership of the "goods" (the slave), whether bought at auction or elsewhere. Sometimes the branding took place *after* a slave had run away or had otherwise misbehaved, to ensure easy identification in the future. In one papyrus dating to 156 B.C. we read of "a runaway branded on the right wrist with two barbaric letters".[3] In this particular document the idea of punishment was absent, but the branding was apparently a mark of ownership.

We cannot help but wonder if Paul, who regarded himself as a slave of Jesus Christ (e.g. Romans 1:1), might not have had this practice of branding in mind as he said that he bore in his body the *stigmata*, the marks of Jesus Christ—for the Greek word he uses at Galatians 6:17 is *stigmata*, translated as "marks". Others could—and did—write of themselves as "a slave of the Emperor",[4] but Paul was privileged to be the slave of the King of Kings. He was serving Him Who had become as a slave for our redemption (Philippians 2:7).

Sometimes a slave was redeemed by a prospective husband, and this was probably the case with a slave girl named Apollonous.[5] Achilleus effected emancipation of the third part of her that was still in slavery, paying a ransom of 200 drachmae of silver. The word "ransom"

47

here is the same as in Matthew 20:28: "Even as the Son of Man came not to be ministered unto, but to minister, and to give His life a *ransom* for many."

This word "ransom"—*lutron*—tells us that Christ came to buy back those who spiritually were slaves. He Who came as a slave (Philippians 2:7), also became the ransom—His life was the redemption price.

There were ways in which slaves could legally gain their freedom—the technical term is "manumission". One early record tells of two Jewish slaves who were set free between 170–157 B.C.—it seems probable they were taken prisoner during the Maccabean wars, and their story was found inscribed on the wall of the Temple of Apollo at Delphi in Achaia.

Selling The Slaves To A God

Manumission on religious grounds was known throughout the areas dominated by the ancient Greek civilization, the practice being nominally to sell the slave to the deity, and then the owner was paid a substantial proportion of what the slave had turned over. Inscriptions show that slaves had been sold in this way to Athene, to Dionysius, to Serapis, to Apollo—and to other gods and goddesses. Jewish people were sometimes included in these religious manumissions, and this is an indication of the Hellenizing compromises accepted by so many Jewish people at these times. As with many people today, these Hellenizers were all too ready to compromise, arguing that the end justified the means.

The actual practice was that the slave managed to save enough money to purchase his own freedom, and so he would come with his owner to the temple where he would be sold to the god. The priests would in turn pay the owner a suitable sum for his having renounced all rights to his property, in the person of the slave. Now that property—the slave himself—was the possession of the god. He was not a slave of the temple, but he came under the protection of that temple's god. As regards other men, including—and indeed especially—his previous master, he was an absolutely free man.

Sometimes there were a few social obligations imposed upon him towards his former master, but these were relatively trivial.

This rite of manumission took place in front of witnesses, and a proper record was kept. It was often inscribed on stone, a sure memorial to the fact that this was a permanent relationship. A great number of these inscriptions were quite simple, naming the slave, and stating that he had been sold to a particular god at a certain price on condition that he was henceforth free: any special arrangements followed, with the names of the selected witnesses.

The Property Of A God—
Never To Be A Slave Again!

Many of the ancient documents of manumission make it extremely clear that under no circumstances would the free man ever be made a slave again, and heavy penalties were prescribed for those who set out to enslave one who had been set free. Against this background it is relevant to read Paul's statement at Galatians 2:4 where he warns against those false brethren who deliberately set out to ensnare believers, to bring them into bondage again. Those false brethren incurred the righteous indignation of the Apostle. Christians are given an incomparable new freedom and they must stand fast and not be "entangled again with the yoke of bondage" (Galatians 5:1).

In this setting the Apostle Paul writes to these Galatian Christians. "O foolish Galatians, who has bewitched you?" he asks (chapter 3:1). "Christ has redeemed us from the curse of the law," he says (verse 13) as he urges these people to accept the vital doctrine of justification by faith in Christ's finished work of redemption. "We are no longer under bondage," he tells them at chapter 4:3, but we are "redeemed from under the law and have received the adoption of sons" (verse 5).

Paul is possibly taking this concept of a slave being sold to the deity and coming under the protection of that god, but he is of course giving it a nobler and deeper spiritual application. Christians enjoyed not simply a

49

nominal association, as with a pagan god of stone, but a new and practical status as adopted sons of the only true God!

Slaves Gain New Citizenship

Even if a man is a slave when he comes to know the Lord, he is the Lord's free man. Natural relationships such as "free man" and "slave" are superseded by the new spiritual relationship in Christ. As our Lord Himself said at John 8:36, "If the Son therefore shall make you free, ye shall be free indeed." He offers a new freedom, such as no man who was merely a citizen of Greece or Rome had ever known before. We have become citizens of Heaven.

Citizens—Yet Slaves!

Yet though the slave becomes a citizen of Heaven, there is a sense in which he accepts a new "slavery". We find in the New Testament that the Christian has the privilege of recognizing himself as the slave of Jesus Christ. Paul himself opened his great Epistle to the Romans by introducing himself as "Paul, a slave of Jesus Christ."

This word *doulos* is usually translated "servant" in the New Testament, but its literal meaning is "slave". In the New Testament a totally new approach is given to slavery because of the concept of the equality of men as they participate in the Kingdom of God. There is an old saying that runs something like this, "Slaves cannot breathe in England: the moment they set foot on its shores they are free." The point is, there is no slavery in England—or in Australia, or many other countries.

It is somewhat like that with Christianity. Once a man becomes a Christian he enters into a new dignity, a relationship of spiritual equality even with his employer. Thus at I Corinthians 12:13 Paul reminds the Christians that they have been baptized into one body by the Holy Spirit, irrespective of whether they were slaves or free men.

In this connection, one of the most interesting New Testament comments on slavery is an indirect one. It is in Romans 16 where we have already seen that slaves are listed as church members in exactly the same way as others of higher social status. They and their Christian masters were brothers in Christ.

Spiritual And Earthly Obligations Of Slaves
At the same time there is a recognition of the social structure and obligations of the times, and so Christian slaves are expected to serve their Christian masters willingly and loyally, and even non-Christian masters are to be given respect. Christian masters, however, are also to treat their slaves well and to recognize that those who are Christians are their brothers in Christ. This is made especially clear in Paul's letter to Philemon, about the latter's runaway slave Onesimus who had been converted and was returning to his master. Paul urged Philemon to receive Onesimus "no longer as a slave . . . but as a brother beloved" (Philemon 16).

"Do Not Drive Us Out!"
In Galatians we find that Satan, the arch-enemy, "troubled" the church in many ways, using people as his agents. As we read a letter from Sarapion to Heraclides,[6] once again we are conscious that we are breathing the same air as did those of New Testament times. "We have many creditors: do not drive us out," we read. The expression, "Do not drive us out," is the same as at Galatians 5:12 where we find that Paul was wishing that the ones *"troubling"* the Christians "were even cut off". The word translated "trouble" is this same word for "driving out". These people were attempting to drive out the influences of Christianity, and so here we have a metaphorical application of this expression which in the papyrus document related to someone driving out another person from his hearth and home. Drs. J. H. Moulton and G. Milligan refer to this papyrus document as an evidence that this word, which was at one time unknown outside Bible writings, was properly used by the New Testament writer. They say, "Its place in the

vernacular is (thus) proved...with singular decisiveness."[7]

If these Galatian Judaizers who sought to re-impose the bondage of the law had been successful, Christians would indeed have been driven out spiritually. But they were wrong, seeking to make a good show before men rather than before God. And that leads to yet another word on which the papyrus has shed light.

Making A Fair Show
One of the words supposedly known only in ecclesiastical writings is at Galatians 6:12, referring to those who desired to make a fair show in the flesh. The Greek word translated "to make a fair show" is *euprosōpeō*, literally meaning "I look well", or "I make a fair show", or even, "My face looks good."

Before this century, Bible commentators suggested that it was not known in secular Greek. However, it has appeared in Egypt in a letter from Pelemon to his brother Menches, dating to 114 B.C. It seems probable that the word was originally a medical term associated with a physical presentation. The medical association is of interest, for in fact Paul uses the term as he discusses those who wrongly insisted on circumcision. However, by the time of this letter the word had come to mean "to make a fair appearance" in the sense of winning the esteem of one's neighbours. Thus, in the Epistle to the Galatians, Paul was probably using the word to mean "winning the good opinion of others".

And in using this—and many other words now recovered from the papyri—Paul was demonstrating the way in which the New Testament writers used the language of ordinary people and contemporary life, even as their Master did before them.

REFERENCES

[1]Oxy. Pap. No. 716.
[2]*J.E.A.* XVII (May 1931), p. 47.
[3]P. Par. No. 10.

[4]Moulton, J. H., and Milligan, G. *The Vocabulary Of The Greek Testament*, p. 170
[5]Oxy. Pap. No. 722.
[6]Milligan, G. *Selections From The Greek Papyri*, p. 38, B.G.U. 1079, A.D. 41.
[7]Moulton, J. H., and Milligan, G. *Ibid.*, p. 38.

4

Christ And His Church

(Ephesians and Colossians)

The Epistles to the Ephesians and to the Colossians are known as "Prison Epistles", and are generally accepted as written during Paul's Roman imprisonment referred to at Acts 28:14–21. Both are dated to A.D. 63. The letter to the Philippians (A.D. 62) and that to Philemon (A.D. 63) were also "Prison Epistles".

The Head And The Body
Ephesians and Colossians were complementary Epistles. Ephesians was probably a letter to be circulated amongst various churches, for some early manuscripts do not include the designation "Ephesus." It was not uncommon for copies of the same writing to be sent to different addresses. The fundamental theme of this Epistle is the unity of the Church, dealing especially with its Divine origin and standing, and the earthly conduct of its members. As it was not called forth to answer local problems or to meet particular circumstances, the Epistle is directed to the Church Universal—and so, in a special sense, to the Church of today.

Differences And Resemblances
There are striking differences between Ephesians and Colossians. Ephesians tells us of our oneness in Christ, whereas Colossians tells us of our completeness in Christ. Ephesians has the Church as its theme: Colossians has Christ. In Ephesians it is the Body; in Colossians the Head. Ephesians has a wonderful revelation, whereas Colossians also contains a great warning concerning false teachers.

However, Colossians also has great resemblances to Ephesians, and in each Epistle the following subjects are dealt with:

Christ is Head of His Church, the Church being His body; He is greater than any angelic beings;

the believer is risen with Christ, being reconciled only because of the death of Christ, and is now made alive with Christ;

Christians are built up as a structure of the Lord, a structure with a sure foundation;

and to them the Divine mystery is revealed.

Of 155 verses in Ephesians, 78 are in Colossians.

The Background Of EKKLĒSIA

Clearly Ephesians and Colossians each deal with Christ and His Church, and in studying these Epistles it is desirable that we should understand something of the word *ekklēsia*, the *"Church".* This is one of the best examples in the New Testament of a spiritual significance being given to a word used in a secular sense, for *ekklēsia* is common enough in ancient Greek, being used in Thucydides and Aristotle. However, it was never used by other people in a religious sense. It referred to a political assembly, or to a city council, or to a parliament.

The religious use of the word comes from the Greek Septuagint (LXX) version of the Old Testament, and in translation this is linked to a Hebrew word *qahal* which has the idea of congregation or assembly. This particular word is seen in the Old Testament at Deuteronomy 5:22, where it is used of the people who are congregated to receive the Law of God. We find it also at I Kings 8:14 (twice) at the dedication of Solomon's Temple, and at Ezra 10:12 as Ezra solemnly reads the Law of God. When Stephen, in New Testament times, referred to these same people—his own nation—he called them "the church (*ekklēsia*) in the wilderness" (Acts 7:38). They were called out from Egypt to a special relationship with God.

From all this we deduce that the people of God were

appointed as *His* people, and were called to Himself. They had the privilege of association with Him in government and even in war. The *ekklēsia* was not merely to be a building, but it was to refer to a people in covenant relationship with God.

This covenant relationship is seen very clearly in the Epistle to the Ephesians, for—as in the Old Testament —the Church is shown by various figures.[1] In the Old Testament the people of God are seen figuratively as Jehovah's bride (Hosea 2:19f.), His vineyard (Isaiah 5:1–7), and even as His child (Hosea 11:1). In Ephesians the *ekklēsia*, the Church, is the Body of Christ (chapter 1:22f.), the Temple of God (chapter 2:21f.), and the Bride of Christ (chapter 5:27–32). This New Testament word *ekklēsia* denotes the people of God, those who are the Israel of the New Covenant (Jeremiah 31:31ff., cf. Hebrews 12:23f., Ephesians 5:25, Matthew 16:17f.).

Our Lord Speaks Of His EKKLĒSIA
Our Lord Himself was the first to associate this word with *His* Church, for we read of it at Matthew 16:18 where Peter had acknowledged that Jesus was the Christ, the Son of the living God. Our Lord told Peter that the Heavenly Father had revealed this truth to him.

The only other occasion where *ekklēsia* is used in the Gospels is at Matthew 18:17. There our Lord says that if a man guilty of sin has refused to repent when he has been told his fault privately, and has continued in his wrong attitude despite the testimony of witnesses, then the matter should be brought before the *ekklēsia*, the Church. This is the assembled gathering of believers.

An extra point is touched on by Drs. Moulton and Milligan. This word, they write, "meant originally any public assembly of citizens summoned by a herald."[2] Relating this to the Church of Jesus Christ—"MY Church"—we marvel as we realize that the convener, the herald, is in a sense God Himself, for He has chosen us in Christ before the foundation of the world (Ephesians 1:4). It is an interesting point on which theologians would differ as to whether our Lord was here distinguishing *His* Church, yet to be built, from the *ekklēsia* of the Old Testament, the Israel of God.

EKKLĒSIA: *A Non-Biblical Word Ennobled*

We saw that at Acts 7:38 the word is also used as a term for Israel. There Stephen referred to the "church (*ekklēsia*) in the wilderness". It is also employed in the Acts in a secular sense. The Town Clerk of Ephesus was very concerned at the great commotion following public accusations laid by the craftsman against Paul, because he was preaching that idols made with hands were not true gods (Acts 19:25–27). A silversmith named Demetrius stirred up the people, claiming that Paul was thus belittling the goddess Diana. The city of Ephesus was supposed to be the "Temple-Keeper of Diana" (a title that the New Testament uses correctly). There was a great uproar, but eventually the Town Clerk quietened the multitude and urged them to have the matter dealt with in the appointed way. When he had thus spoken "he dismissed the *ekklēsia*"—the assembly.

In fact, the word is well-known in early non-Biblical writings, and perhaps one of the most interesting illustrations is an inscription dated to A.D. 103 in Ephesus—the very city with which it is associated in Acts 19. This particular inscription relates to the presentation of a silver image of the goddess Diana by a Roman official, C. Vibius Salutaris. He also gave other images—"that they might be set up in every *ekklēsia* ..."

However, we see that in the New Testament this word *ekklēsia* has been dignified and spiritualized by association with Christ's Church.

Literary Forms About Prayer

We come to the Epistles—Ephesians and Colossians—themselves.

Paul commenced his letters in the way common to his times, as is attested in many papyrus records. Even his giving thanks to God is somewhat similar to pagan expressions. In chapter 2 we referred to the Egyptian soldier Apion who wrote to his father Epimachus in the 2nd century A.D. "I thank the lord Serapis," he says, giving praise to his false god. In doing so he reminds us of Paul's expression of thanks to the true God, as at Ephesians 1:16, and at various other places in his letters (e.g. I Thessalonians 1:2; Philemon 4; Romans 1:8; Philippians 1:3).

In this same verse (Ephesians 1:16) Paul assures his Christian friends of his constant intercession for them. Our same soldier Apion wrote a letter to his sister Sabina —"Before all things I pray that thou art in health, for I also am in health, *making mention of thee* before the gods here . . ." Paul also says that he "ceases not to give thanks for you, *making mention of you* in my prayers".

Paul writes to the Christians at Thessalonica and at Rome, and we learn that he *makes mention of them* all in prayer. And when we come to the last letter of this great Apostle, the Second Epistle to Timothy, he says that he *makes unceasing mention of Timothy* in his supplications. The Apostle Paul had come to know the true God, and he spent many an hour interceding on behalf of the young Christian Church over which he had such special responsibilities.

The False And The True
On this matter of prayer, the two-fold similarity from ancient letters is interesting—there is prayer to the deity as a necessary part of life, and there is the assurance that this prayer is made on behalf of those addressed. The use of such expressions as "making mention of you" in both secular and sacred writings is a further indication of the contemporary nature of the New Testament documents.

The literary form is similar, but what a difference there is in reality of experience and sincerity of approach! This is even seen in the language used. Apion's letter to one of his own blood was rather cold and formal, but Paul—writing to those *not* related by blood but made one in Christ—is warm, personal, sincere. Paul wrote of a loving Heavenly Father interested in each of His people, and not just of vague impersonal gods who must be placated. Apion had a form of godliness that lacked power. He merely scribbled a formal declaration as to an intercession which was ritualistic, with but little faith in the "prayer" being answered. What did the gods (plural in the second letter) care about the health of Sabina, the insignificant sister of a second century Egyptian enrolled in the Roman army?

"Releasing" From Our Sins

Another notable word which Paul uses is *aphesis*, which refers to forgiveness. This word is used at many places in the New Testament, our present example being at Ephesians 1:7, where we are told of our redemption through the blood of Jesus Christ, "the forgiveness of sins."

Aphesis appears in the papyrus fragments, associated with water being "released" from the canal so that the fields can be irrigated. That water is not brought back into the canals, but is forever gone. So it is with a person who is forgiven. He is "released" from his sins and they will not be held against him again.

The word also occurs in inscriptions referring to debts being paid off in full, and also as to punishment being completely remitted. Similarly, a crop was "released" when the taxes had been paid, and so it was available for disposal by the cultivator. Each of these activities can be related to a person who knows forgiveness by Jesus Christ and has his debt of sins cancelled. The penalty is completely remitted because it has been borne in the Person of the Lord Jesus Christ Who offered Himself for our sins according to the Scriptures. We are *released* from them.

Citizens Of Heaven

Another concept in Ephesians is "citizenship"—the Greek word *politeuma*. "You are no longer strangers and foreigners, but fellow-citizens of the saints, and of the household of God," Paul writes (Ephesians 2:19). We have said that Ephesians was actually a circular letter, going beyond one city such as Ephesus. Christians everywhere were given a new citizenship, not of Ephesus, but of Heaven itself.

The verb form of the same word is used at Philippians 1:27 which is translated in the Authorized Version, "Let your *conversation* be as it becometh the gospel of Christ." Here the meaning is "to behave as a citizen . . ." (See also Philippians 3:20—"our *conversation*—our citizenship—is in heaven.") The Christian has a new citizenship, going beyond earthly relationships or national loyalties. He is already a citizen of Heaven. And the price paid was infinitely greater than that paid for any other citizenship. *Our* citizenship cost the Son of Man His life.

This is seen more clearly when we understand the background. Citizenship was not lightly attained in the Roman Empire. That is demonstrated by the comment of a Roman centurion to the Apostle Paul when Paul demanded his rights as a Roman citizen. The centurion said to Paul, "With a great sum I obtained this freedom" (Acts 22:28). "But I was free-born," Paul replied. Elsewhere he tells us that he was "a citizen of no mean city" (Acts 21:39), that city being Tarsus in Cilicia.

Citizenship of a city was granted on occasions for services to the Romans—e.g. in times of war. It could also be bought, at a very high price. There are recorded instances of this being a lucrative "side-income" for the Imperial family.

In the main, Jewish people were not Roman citizens, and many—though by no means all—of the early Christians were Jewish.

New Privileges
Jews were unable to share many of the social activities of those around them, but they did enjoy special privileges, both under the Hellenistic rulers and later under the Romans. The Romans continued these privileges, partly because of the difficulty of maintaining control over the Jews who always insisted that their particular religious scruples be tolerated.

The Jews were not satisfied with the privileges they

60

were given, and it is an historical fact that they did their utmost to gain greater benefits. One example of this in the 1st century A.D. was when they made great efforts—though unsuccessfully—to win full citizenship rights in Alexandria. Certain concessions were granted to them, but they were always suspect and as a people never obtained the full rights they demanded. However, in a sense they gained more than citizenship in that they were allowed their own synagogue council, and had the right to deal with many of their own special problems.

But Jewish people were desperately unhappy under the Romans—as shown by the communities who fled for relief out to the barren areas near the Dead Sea.

Many of the non-Jewish Christians also groaned under the bondage of Rome. They could not afford to buy citizenship rights, and their lot was difficult indeed. Very often they were slaves, with practically no personal liberty at all.*

Against these backgrounds—Jewish and Gentile alike —the Christian message as to a new citizenship was especially relevant. That new citizenship conferred privileges beyond anything Rome could ever offer. They were "fellow-citizens" of Heaven, and theirs was an eternal relationship which no Caesar or foreign overlord could alter.

The Important Role Of Ambassador
Indeed, the Christian is not only a "fellow-citizen". He has the honour of representing the King of Kings, as a special "ambassador".

At Ephesians 6:20 Paul says he is "an ambassador in bonds". He uses this same word (*presbeuō*) at II Corinthians 5:20 where he includes other Christian workers in this category as he declares, "Now then, we are *ambassadors* for Christ, as though God did beseech you by us: we pray you in Christ's stead, be ye reconciled to God."

Paul the Roman citizen is here referring to a Roman

*See Chapter 3.

office, using it to give a spiritual lesson, emphasizing the privileged position of those presenting the claims of Jesus Christ. An "ambassador" was a legate of the emperor—a highly responsible representative of the Caesar. By the parallel we are reminded of *our* spiritual privilege as we present the gospel message. We are not merely representatives of a petty Caesar whose voice would soon be silent, but we are ambassadors of the Emperor of Emperors. And so we beseech men, in Christ's stead, "Be reconciled to God."

Refuting The Heresy Of Angel Worship

At the beginning of this chapter we said that Ephesians has the Church as a major theme, whereas Colossians places more emphasis on the Person of Our Lord Himself. One of the most important aspects of Colossians is its insistence on the true humanity and the absolute Deity of the Lord Jesus Christ.

We saw that Judaizing was dealt with especially in the Epistle to the Galatians, but in Colossians an early form of gnosticism is refuted.* Gnostics emphasized knowledge as the essential thing, and regarded matter as evil. They rejected the possibility of Christ being in a body of flesh, and claimed that God could be reached only through a series of angelic emanations whereby the problems of the flesh could be overcome by a process, instead of in one direct step from God to man. This led to the worship of angels, with Christ Himself regarded as little more than another angel (Colossians 2:18, 19).

Christ's Absolute Deity

Gnostics also regarded Christ as Divine in a limited sense, but not absolute in His Deity. "No," said Paul to the Colossians, "In *Him* dwelleth *all* the fulness of the Godhead *bodily*" (chapter 2:9). He used the Greek word *sōmatikōs*, making clear the physical nature of Christ's flesh and at the same time equally insisting on His

*See *New Light On The Gospels*, chapter 4.

absolute Deity. Paul also clearly rejected both angel worship (chapter 2:18) and wrongful punishment of the flesh (verses 20, 21). Rather he stressed the need for self-control as regards wrong desires (chapter 3:5ff.).

Strangely enough, this heretical teaching regarding matter as evil led to two opposite practices. On one hand there was rigid asceticism whereby the body was maltreated because it was supposedly evil—and the Colossian heretics emphasized this aspect. On the other hand there was unbridled licence, for there were those who said that what took place in the body was simply the result of man's unfortunate make-up, and he was not responsible for his flesh. This led to something akin to an Epicurean philosophy in its worst expressions of "eat, drink and be merry". Indeed, it went beyond true Epicurean notions, for to the Epicurean pleasure was the end to be desired, but that pleasure was not necessarily a short-lived thing. It could involve self-discipline and restriction of fleshly indulgence, because in the long run such restraint might lead to the most satisfaction.

Christ The First-Born

Another subject in Colossians relating to the Lord Jesus Christ is the use of the Greek word *prōtotokos*, "first-born." J. H. Thayer* quoted this as one of the words regarded as "Biblical"—supposedly not known outside the Bible. However, it has been found on the tomb of a pagan high priest, and also on an epitaph in Rome dating to the 2nd or 3rd century A.D. The word is again used relating to a child who died when only two years of age.

In the first-mentioned of these inscriptions we learn that the man was a priest by the rights of the *first-born*, and it seems probable that in this particular family the first-born had the office of priest. This is paralleled in many an Eastern family today, as in India where the writer has personally known of the first-born son exercising priestly functions for the family. This ancient

*See *New Light On The Gospels*, chapters 6 and 9.

practice, where the first-born and the priest were identified, leads to the concept of superiority.

In the Bible, "first-born" and "first-begotten" do not
necessarily mean born first in the sense of time. A
comparison of the Scriptures as to the birth of Abraham
makes it clear that he was not literally the first-born of
the sons of Terah, but he was the spiritual leader of the
family, and so in the Biblical record he is placed first.
Similarly we read about Ephraim and Manasseh at
Genesis 48:8–22. Manasseh was the first-born son of
Joseph, but Jacob gave the blessing to Ephraim, and he
became the leader in the sense of spiritual superiority.
In this connection it is interesting to read the comment
at Jeremiah 31:9, "Ephraim is my first-born."

The importance and rights of the first-born are also
seen as Esau sold his birthright to Jacob.

Others Restored To Life

And so, when we come to the New Testament, we find
that the Lord Jesus Christ is referred to as "the first-born
from the dead" (Colossians 1:18), and the word *prōtotokos* is used. The Lord Jesus Christ was not the first to
rise from the dead in point of time: had not both Elijah
and Elisha raised the dead, and did not the Lord Jesus
Himself raise Lazarus? It is true of course that He is
"the first-born from the dead" in that He is the first to
have passed through death, never to die again.

However, the verse in Colossians is a reference to the
superiority of the One Who Himself was and is the
Life. In the sense of His *pre-eminence* He is the first-born
of every creature (Colossians 1:15): He is the superior
One, pre-eminent amongst all those who have ever been
born. Thus these statements in no way take from the
uniqueness or the Deity of the Lord Jesus Christ, but
they are simply declarations as to His pre-eminence.

Christ is the first-born from the dead. His death was
to give us life, and He was "raised again for our justification" (Romans 4:25). He has redeemed us from death,
the penalty for sin.

The Handwriting Nailed To The Cross

Another word which is used to show that Christ has redeemed us is that employed by the Apostle Paul at Colossians 2:14, where he speaks of "the *handwriting* of ordinances against us". This word, *cheirographon* or "handwriting", is actually a technical word referring to a memorandum of debt. Christ has paid the debt against us. As we read that this "memorandum of debt" was nailed to His cross, we are reminded that the receipt was displayed publicly so that none could argue that the debt was yet to be paid. The price of our redemption was declared by His public crucifixion.

It is known that it was a custom in antiquity to cancel a debt by crossing it out with the Greek letter *chi* which is in the form of an "X"—a cross, and there is very possibly a play on words here as Paul says that Christ has taken our debt and nailed it to the cross. However, there is the deeper significance to which we have already referred–the public display of Himself as a final evidence that the debt was paid.

In the so-called Florentine Papyrus there is a fragment dating to A.D. 85 in which a trial is taking place and the Governor of Egypt gives an order, "Let the handwriting be crossed out"—and so the debt was cancelled and the case was settled.

Was A Document Nailed To The Doorway?

We realize it is sometimes stated that the practice was for a document to be nailed to a debtor's doorpost—e.g. in this connection we have before us a quotation to that effect by the late Dr. A. T. Pierson in his fascinating papers, *Jesus Christ and the Two Testaments*. As far as we know this tradition is unconfirmed from ancient sources.

The following comment in the I.V.F. *New Bible Commentary* at p. 1048 is typical of authoritative statements as to this supposed practice:

"The suggestion that the reference is to the cancellation of a debt by running a nail through it and displaying it in

E

a public place is not convincing. No evidence of such a custom exists."

However, in his famous commentary Bishop Ellicott made an extra point that there could be an indirect allusion to the "title" which would have been nailed to the cross of Christ.

. . . .

And so we have glanced at some of the ways in which ancient writings have touched on matters raised in Ephesians and Colossians. We have seen the ennoblement of language in a word such as *ekklēsia*, but especially we have been reminded of the new relationship because Christ—"in Whom dwelleth all the fulness of the Godhead bodily"–took away the "handwriting of ordinances that were against us, nailing it to His cross" (Colossians 2:14).

REFERENCES

[1]Furness, J. M. *Vital Words Of The Bible*, p. 47f. for further discussion.
[2]Moulton, J. H., and Milligan, G. *The Vocabulary Of The Greek Testament*, p. 195.

5

Counting All Things Loss And Gaining New Status

(*Philippians and Philemon*)

In this chapter we look briefly at the Epistles to the Philippians and to Philemon, each of which Paul wrote as a prisoner. Elsewhere (Romans 1:1) he refers to himself as a slave, and in Philemon he writes to a slave-owner concerning a runaway slave Onesimus who had been converted. The slave now gains a new status, for he and his master Philemon have become brothers in Christ.

PART I: ON COUNTING ALL THINGS LOSS
(*Philippians 3:8*)
We come then to the Epistle to the Philippians.

One of the most thrilling stories in the New Testament is in this Epistle, though it is not told in great detail—we refer to the way Epaphroditus struggled through to the Apostle Paul at the risk of his own life. In this same Epistle we read that Paul himself was prepared to suffer the loss of everything in the service of Christ (chapter 3:7ff.), and Epaphroditus displayed the same spirit. He was bringing a love-gift from the beloved church at Philippi, a church which had repeatedly been faithful in giving to others, as the Apostle Paul himself says at chapter 4:15.

Paul goes on to say that the Philippians had "sent once and again unto my necessity". Now their representative Epaphroditus had risked his own life to bring their gift —it was "an odour of a sweet smell, a sacrifice acceptable, well-pleasing to God" (chapter 4:18). These poverty-stricken Christians gave of their very substance.

"My God Shall Supply All Your Need"

It is in this context that we read that heartening verse, "But my God shall supply all your need according to His riches in glory by Christ Jesus" (chapter 4:19). Paul was writing to those who had provided for him out of—and despite—their own poverty. They themselves had given fruit that would abound to their account (verse 17), and they could accept as their own the assurance Paul now gave, that God would indeed make it up to them —He would supply all *their* need. This was a promise given especially to those who in obedience and love had already given sacrificially to provide the needs of others. (How often it is quoted out of context to missionaries today by those who have *not* sacrificially given!)

No Murmurings–No Disputings!

It has often been pointed out that this generous Philippian church was in some ways a "model church" as to its display of Christian love. The only hint of any friction at all is where Paul beseeches two women "to be of the same mind in the Lord" (Philippians 4:2).

However, Paul knew full well that disputes could come all too easily—indeed, when all is running smoothly is often the time for special care. Perhaps this is one reason why we read his exhortation, "Do all things without *murmurings* (*goggusmōn*) and disputings" (chapter 2:14).

The papyrus documents throw a little extra light on this word "murmurings". From the papyrus at Oxyrhynchus we learn that while the emperor was sitting in judgment the Romans were *murmuring*—they were discontented with the authorities over them, and so they *murmured*. Christians are not to murmur against God Who is their Heavenly Sovereign, nor are they to be unnecessarily involved in disputes with others.

On Risking One's Life

But let us go back to Epaphroditus—a common enough name in the Roman era. One document dating to A.D. 182 tells of a slave named Epaphroditus, aged only eight years, who leaned out of a bedroom, fell, and was killed[1] —reminding us of the incident of Eutychus whom Paul raised to life (Acts 20:9f.). In another papyrus letter, dating to 2 B.C., we find that another Epaphroditus has not received certain money that had been sent to him.

We read at Philippians 2:25–27 that the New Testament Epaphroditus was "sick nigh unto death", and Paul tells the Philippians that they should hold him in honour because "for the work of Christ he was nigh unto death, not regarding his life, to supply your lack of service towards me" (verse 30).

In this verse Paul uses the Greek word *paraboleuomai* which literally means "I expose myself". The root word conveys the thought of being venturesome. Although it was earlier thought to be known only in the Bible, it has been found in an inscription at Olbia on the Black Sea, where a man named Carzoazus is praised for the way he had, in somewhat similar fashion, "exposed himself." This particular man had "exposed himself to danger" as the legal advocate of his clients, at times taking personal risks when he brought his client's cause to the court of the emperor. In this case the New Testament usage of the word was a help to the translators at this point, making clear the meaning of the word as it is used in this inscription.

We read that this legal man's reputation in this way extended through "all the world". Thus our Black Sea inscription also throws light on an expression at Romans 1:8, "Your faith is spoken of *throughout the whole world*." The Greek idiom used at this verse is put differently from that in the inscription, but each uses the expression "through all the world". The use of hyperbole in this way was quite common in Eastern lands such as those of the New Testament.

It would be interesting to know if Paul himself knew that *his* faith would be spoken of through the world, and down through the centuries. His desire to know "Christ and Him crucified" has been echoed in the hearts of thousands who have been encouraged by his utter devotion.

On Laying Down One's Neck

The preparedness of Epaphroditus to expose himself to danger reminds us of Aquila and Priscilla who also had been willing to risk their lives for Paul's sake, and at Romans 16:4 we read his commendation of them: "Who have for my life *laid down their own necks:* unto whom not only I give thanks, but also all the churches of the Gentiles."

Jews had been banished from Rome by the edict of Claudius in A.D. 52, and this couple, Aquila and Priscilla, had been included in the ban, as shown in Acts 18:1, 2. However, before Paul wrote this letter to the Romans, Christians were able to return, and Aquila and Priscilla had gone back to the capital.

Over the years commentators have differed as to the meaning of this expression, "laid down their necks." Because the Roman means of execution was by the axe, many have suggested that Aquila and Priscilla had been sentenced to be beheaded. Others have believed that the expression was to be taken in a figurative sense, to convey the idea that they were prepared to die if necessary rather than desert or betray their beloved Paul. It seems best to see the expression as a parallel to the English colloquialism "to risk one's neck". A similar usage can be seen also in Romans 16:4.

Light From Herculaneum

An almost identical expression comes from the city of Herculaneum. This city and Pompeii were both buried under lava in the year A.D. 79. Not only were the citizens of these places overtaken suddenly, but so also were the people's libraries, and now some of these have been recovered. In one of them was a biography of an Epicurean—a Greek philosopher named Philonides who lived about 230 years before the city of Herculaneum was destroyed. We do not know who it was who wrote the story of this ancient philosopher, but of course he must have written before the city itself was devastated. In passing we may note that so long ago citizens had their libraries, and that in ancient times biographies were written of men of previous generations.

But our special interest in this biography from Herculaneum is that in it we have this expression: "For the most beloved of his relatives or friends he would readily stake his neck." The verb is different, but the basic expression and meaning are the same. The original idea was that somebody who was prepared to die as a substitute for a friend ought to be responsible before the law for that person, even it meant that his own life was forfeit.

The letter from Herculaneum indicates that the expression "lay down their necks" should be taken colloquially, but it also points to the great affection between Paul and his friends Aquila and Priscilla. Obviously it would only be for the most beloved of friends that one would be prepared to lay down his life.

Yet another relevant papyrus dates to the early 2nd century B.C. and is a severe rebuke addressed to a minor official named Dionysius: "You should play the fool at the risk of your own neck, and not of mine!"[2] Dionysius had been guilty of drinking while on duty, but had not taken into account the consequences, and so this letter of rebuke was sent to him.

Aquila and Priscilla, Epaphroditus and Paul—each of them was willing to go into death if need be for the cause of Jesus Christ. They were determined to present Jesus Christ and Him crucified.

Bones For The Dogs
Paul makes his determination to serve Christ abundantly clear at Philippians 3:7, 8, where he uses a strong word to tell us that those things which were gain to him he counted *loss* for Christ. He goes on to say that he "counts all things but *loss* for the excellency of the knowledge of Christ Jesus my Lord: for Whom I have suffered the *loss* of all things". Three times the Apostle uses one or another form of *zēmia*, meaning "loss".

This word is used in an ancient papyrus relating to refuse—in this document the refuse being bones that have been thrown out to the dogs in the street. Paul is telling us that whatever loss he has suffered is as refuse —it is as nothing compared with the great gain that is his through the knowledge of Christ Jesus his Lord.

A verb form of that word *zēmia* was also used in 153 B.C. by a man named Apollonius concerning a runaway slave who has been recovered and *fined* fifteen bronze talents.[3] At first sight it might seem strange to think of an association between the word "fine" and "loss" as they are in our English language. But Apollonius was referring to the cost to the slave, and in a similar way the "fine" or "cost" that the Apostle Paul paid was the loss of all things—not just fifteen bronze talents.

He expresses a similar thought in another way at Romans 8:18: "For I reckon that the sufferings of this present time are not worthy to be compared with the glory which shall be revealed in us."

PART II: ON GAINING NEW STATUS
(The Epistle To Philemon)

Though written at about the same time as Philippians, the Epistle of Paul to Philemon follows Titus in the New Testament, and again we find interesting light from the papyri. One letter is from a man named Caor, a village priest at the town of Hermupolis in ancient Egypt. He writes to a Roman officer in the Fayum concerning a runaway soldier whose name was Paul: "Pardon him this once, seeing that I am without leisure to come unto thee at this present."

It seems that this soldier had made the village priest his confidante, and now the priest becomes the intercessor. It is somewhat similar to what we find in the story of Onesimus, the runaway slave for whom Paul pleads to his friend Philemon—that is the basis of this letter to Philemon. It is one of the most delightfully human stories in the Bible.

One surprising aspect of this New Testament letter of only one chapter is that it is virtually a letter of commendation, in that the slave's owner is asked to welcome home the truant as though he were a special

72

friend—"Receive him ... as a brother beloved," Paul urges (verses 15, 16).

Paul himself had apparently been the agent in Onesimus' eternal salvation (verse 10), and now he urges the slave's master to look on his slave as a partner—"If thou count me therefore a partner, receive him as myself" (verse 17). This was an amazing request.

Something similar—though not concerning a slave—is found in a 2nd century A.D. letter, this time written in Latin, and found at Oxyrhynchus. It is to the military Tribune Julius Domitius, from his benefactor Aurelius Archelaus. Among other things the Tribune's benefactor writes: "Already aforetime I have recommended unto thee Theon my friend, and now also I pray, lord, that thou mightest have him before thine eyes as myself."

The benefactor addresses the Tribune as "lord," this simply being a polite salutation. Theon was entitled to commendation, for as we read on we find that "he left his own people, his goods and business, and followed me. And through all things he hath kept me in safety".

A Slave—But "Free Indeed"

We can understand that the Tribune should be asked to treat Theon as the special representative and friend of his benefactor, but such a commendation—of a slave—can be understood in the New Testament letter only on spiritual grounds. For Onesimus the slave had become converted to Jesus Christ. He had become, spiritually, a brother to his earthly master Philemon. The slave had been "made free indeed" (John 8:36).

There is a measure of similarity between Aurelius Archelaus and Julius Domitius on the one hand, and the Apostle Paul and Philemon on the other. In a sense Paul was Philemon's "benefactor", for Philemon owed to Paul the wonder of redemption through Christ. Paul reminded Philemon, "Albeit I do not say to thee how thou owest unto me even thine own self besides" (verse 19).

73

"Charge It To My Account!"

Paul also writes to Philemon, "If he hath wronged thee, or oweth thee ought, put that on my account" (verse 18).

This particular injunction by Paul contains yet another word that was supposedly used only in the Scripture— the Greek word *ellogeō*, which literally means "I charge to someone's account". The word has been found in an edict issued by the Roman Emperor Diocletian, and again in an even earlier imperial letter dating to the time of the Emperor Hadrian. In this letter the Emperor is anxious to avoid any appearance of having imposed an obligation, or of "charging to the account" of the soldiers, any benefits that had been granted to them. This "charging to their account" is the same word the Apostle Paul used at Philemon verse 18—Paul is telling Philemon that if the fugitive slave Onesimus owed his master anything, this should be "charged to my account".

Similarly at Romans 5:13 the word is again used, though this time in a more abstract sense. Paul writes, "For until the law sin was in the world; but sin is not *imputed* when there is no law." The word translated "imputed" in the Authorized Version is again *ellogeō* —"to put to one's account," and so Paul is saying that sin was not charged against one's account when there was no law.

But let us go back to Philemon. Another ancient letter is that from Demophon, a wealthy Egyptian, to Ptolemaeus, a police official, which Dr. B. P. Grenfell and Dr. A. S. Hunt published. The letter reads in part: "And if it is necessary to spend anything, pay it. Thou shalt receive it from us . . ." How similar that is to the language Paul used about that runaway slave! "I will repay it," said Paul—and surely *his* guarantee was as acceptable as that of the wealthy Demophon! Such words must have given real hope to Onesimus, now surrendering himself to his master Philemon.

REFERENCES

[1]Baikie, J. *Egyptian Papyri And Papyrus-Hunting*, pp. 285f.

[2]Hunt, A. S., and Smyly, J. G. *The Tebtunis Papyri*, Volume III, Part I, p. 179.
[3]Milligan, G. *Selections From The Greek Papyri*, p. 22, P. Par. No. 47.

6

The King's Return
In Triumph

(I and II Thessalonians)

Because the Epistle to the Romans appears early in the New Testament, many Christians think of it as the first letter that Paul wrote, but his earliest letters in the Canon are I and II Thessalonians.

They are sometimes referred to as the prophetic Epistles, containing as they do so much about Christ's return—the Christian's hope. They were written during Paul's second missionary journey, details of which are recorded at Acts 15:36–18:22. This journey is dated from A.D. 51 to A.D. 54. Scholars usually date I Thessalonians to A.D. 52, and II Thessalonians to A.D. 53.

Christ's Second Coming
In I Thessalonians Paul wrote to reassure believers as to the eternal hope of those who died before Christ's second advent, and in each chapter he referred to this, the great hope of the Christian.

The Second Epistle again has the second coming of Christ as its central theme, and a major purpose was to correct false ideas as to that return.

As he writes of Christ's second advent, Paul uses the word *parousia*. This is the Greek for "coming", and the Lord used this word in answer to a question from the disciples as to when His Kingdom would be manifested (Matthew 24:3).

The word is also found in the papyrus from Egypt. In its early uses it simply meant "coming", but by New Testament times it had a technical meaning, referring to great occasions such as the visit of a king or some other very distinguished person. A deputation of the leading citizens would go out to meet the king and escort him in royal procession back into the city. Christ's *parousia* will be a most glorious occasion, for this will be the appearance of the King of Kings.

The "Manifestation" Of Deity

This word *parousia* is closely tied to another cult word, *epiphaneia*, and the two ideas are associated in the New Testament at II Thessalonians 2:8. In the Pastoral Epistles *epiphaneia* usually refers to the second *parousia* of Christ, though at II Timothy 1:10 it relates to His first appearance.

In Hellenistic times one way in which the word *epiphaneia* was used was as to the supposed manifestation of the gods, this being involved in the blasphemous title which Antiochus Epiphanes took to himself. Antiochus was claiming to be a manifestation of deity—as an incarnation of the Greek god Zeus. It was Antiochus who caused the Jewish temple and other altars in Judea to be desecrated, leading to the Maccabean Revolt in the 2nd century B.C. The true Jew could not acknowledge the "manifestation" or "appearance" of any pagan god. There was only one God, Jehovah.

Two PAROUSIAS And The Papyri

We have said that Christ actually has two *parousias*, and this is part of the thought behind the text at Zechariah 9:9 and Matthew 21:5: "Behold thy King cometh unto thee." In His time of rejection there were those who acknowledged Him as the King of Kings, even as He rode into Jerusalem on a donkey. This was indeed the first *parousia* of the King of Kings. It is His second *parousia* which is so prominent in the two Epistles to the Thessalonians.

Even the possibility of two *parousias* has light thrown on it from the recovered writings. One inscription dating to A.D. 124 referred to more than one *parousia* in Greece of the god Hadrian.[1] At Christ's first *parousia* He came

77

unto His own and His own received Him not. The King of Kings was then given a crown of thorns, but He has since been crowned King in the lives of hundreds of thousands of His followers who "see Jesus, *crowned* with glory and honour" (Hebrews 2:9). And in an even fuller sense He will be acknowledged in a coming day. Every knee shall bow before Him. (Philippians 2:10; Hebrews 1:8; Revelation 11:15.)

The Costs Of Royal Visits

Needless to say, great costs were associated with the *parousia* of a visiting dignitary, and these had to be borne by the people. Special taxes were levied, and various other payments were expected. In Greece itself a new era was commenced from the *parousia* of the Emperor Hadrian, in that from that time "advent" coins were struck all over the world to commemorate the *parousia* of the emperor.

One inscription from Olbia on the Black Sea, dating to the 3rd century A.D., tells of the *parousia* of King Saitapharnes, and the city fathers were very concerned at how the expense could be met. Then a rich citizen, Protogenes, paid the total amount of nine hundred pieces of gold. This was in turn presented to the king, to the great relief of the city fathers!

Sir Flinders Petrie quotes a papyrus dating to the 3rd century B.C.[2] in which contributions are referred to for an amount of gold presented to the king at his *parousia*. In another papyrus[3] the Emperor Claudius writes, "I received with pleasure the golden crowns as an expression of your loyal devotion towards me." But though the Sovereigns of the world expected costly crowns at the expense of the people, at the *parousia* of the Lord Jesus Christ His saints also are to be given crowns of glory.

A petition dating to about 113 B.C. was found in the wrappings of a sacred crocodile. It tells of a requisition for corn because of the forthcoming *parousia* of Ptolemy II. Interestingly enough, this Ptolemy called himself Soter which means "saviour". In a sense this was blasphemous, for only Jesus Christ is the true Saviour.

An inscription dating to the 3rd century A.D. shows that *parousia* was sometimes used in a religious sense, for it talks of a cure at the temple of Asclepius at Epidaurus, and says this healing is the result of the *parousia* of the healer god (Asclepius). In the background of the New Testament there was a longing, a searching for the appearance of the true God.

This is seen in its fullest spiritual significance as Paul tells the Thessalonians that their hope will be realized at the appearance of the true God and Saviour, even Jesus Christ.

We find this word *parousia* is used at various places such as I Thessalonians 2:19: "For what is our hope, or joy, or crown of rejoicing? Are not even ye in the presence of our Lord Jesus Christ at His *coming?*" His "coming" is His *parousia*—His Royal Presence.

The Giving Of Crowns
We saw that at their *parousia* the kings of the world were given costly crowns for themselves, but that at the *parousia* of the Lord Jesus Christ those who have served Him will also be given crowns. At our verse in I Thessalonians 2:19 we read of the Christian's crown, and II Timothy 4:8 makes it clear that a crown will be given to all those who "love His appearing". The word *epiphaneia* is used here for "appearing", and we saw that it means "manifestation", but a similar thought is also expressed at I Thessalonians 3:13 where we read of the "coming" (*parousia*) of our Lord Jesus Christ, with all His saints. Theological argument as to the exact sequence of events is outside the purpose of this survey. In any case, time becomes unimportant as we enter these realms of eternity. The truth is that His saints *will* reign with Christ!

As he nears the end of his life Paul puts it like this: "I have fought a good fight, I have finished my course, I have kept the faith; henceforth there is laid up for me a crown of righteousness" (II Timothy 4:7f.).

One of the inscriptions in the British Museum has this comment: "He fought three fights and twice was crowned." Paul was using a figure of speech from his own times—but how much surer the reward was for the Christian! For in *this* warfare the one who "overcomes" will be seated with the King, on His throne (Revelation 3:21).

"Comfort One Another"

There are of course other important subjects dealt with in Thessalonians besides our Lord's *parousia*, and we have said that one of Paul's purposes in writing I Thessalonians was to reassure the believers as to their eternal hope.

One melancholy letter written in the 2nd century A.D. illustrates the difference in hope between Christians and non-Christians. It is from a lady named Irene—a word meaning "peace"—to a family in mourning over a child who died. The letter is actually addressed to a married couple, the man being Philo—a name that is based on a Greek word which means "I love".

This letter reminds us how unchanging human emotions are, for Irene writes to say that though she has done all that is required of her in official mourning yet "nevertheless against such things one can do nothing".

There is a considerable similarity in Irene's closing exhortation—"Therefore, comfort ye one another"—with that of the Apostle Paul in I Thessalonians 4:18—"Wherefore comfort one another with these words." The wording is not exactly the same in Greek, but the thought forms are very similar.

However, there is an essential spiritual difference, for Irene is resigned to the awfulness of death, mankind's inevitable lot; a prospect unrelieved by any hope of life beyond the grave. But the Apostle Paul has a note of victory in a great climax which triumphs over death. His "comfort" centres in the realization of a new beginning beyond death. The Christian message which Paul declared shone with hope, and so was full of true "comfort".

A Comment On Paul's Self-Defence

Another purpose of Paul's writing his first letter to the Thessalonians was to defend himself against false charges laid by jealous Jews (I Thessalonians 2:3–9). There is also a measure of self-defence in his second letter, as at II Thessalonians 3:7 where he reminds the Christians that he and his fellow-workers did not *behave in any disorderly way*, and he went on to say, "Neither did we eat any man's bread for nought; but wrought with labour and travail night and day, that we might not be chargeable to any of you."

To "behave disorderly" is from a Greek word *atakteō*, which commonly means "to be idle" and, as it is used here, implies disorderly behaviour because of idleness. This meaning is illustrated from a contract of apprenticeship dating to A.D. 66.[4] The word refers to the possibility of the boy *being idle*, or it could even mean "playing truant". The boy is to extend his apprenticeship by an equal number of days as the days he did not work.

It is interesting to find *atakteō* in such a setting—and this is not the only example—where the boy concerned is to work extra time to ensure that there is no possibility of his having imposed on his master. Otherwise, the contract states, he is to pay back a silver drachma for each day lost.

Against this background the statement of Paul gains extra sense. Christians are not to impose on each other, and the Apostle set a clear example by working so diligently with his own hands. The false claims of those who opposed him were refuted.

REFERENCES

[1] Deissmann, A. *Light From The Ancient East*, p. 372.
[2] *Ibid.*, p. 373.
[3] Pap. Lond. 1178.
[4] Oxy. Pap. No. 275.

F

7

The Last Letters
Of A Great Man

(I and II Timothy and Titus)

We come to the last letters in the New Testament of this great man Paul—written in prison, probably chained to a Roman soldier even while he dictated to an amanuensis.

Paul's two letters to Timothy and the one to Titus are usually referred to as the Pastoral Epistles, outlining as they do the duties of Christian workers. The early Church readily accepted their Pauline authorship and their place in the Canon. In the second century well-known writers such as Ignatius, Polycarp, Irenaeus, Tertullian and Clement of Alexandria accepted them as genuine Apostolic Epistles. In these Epistles Paul does not deal with some problems frequently associated with pastoral responsibilities, the reason no doubt being that he had already given attention to many such matters in his earlier letters.

Paul had such an affection for these two younger men who in a special sense are to carry on the work, that he writes to them as "Timothy, a true child in the faith" and "Titus, a true child according to the common faith". In each case Paul uses the Greek word *gnēsios*, meaning "true" or "genuine", and this is the word used in a marriage contract where someone is legally wedded. In the very first of the so-called Elephantine Papyri we read of a man called Heroclides who takes Demetria as his *lawful* wife—his *true* wife. This is one of the earliest of the papyrus fragments, dating as it does to 311 B.C.

Drs. Moulton and Milligan discuss this word *gnēsios* and show that its primary meaning was "born in wedlock", but that this became overshadowed by derived applications. Thus it had a variety of additional meanings such as legal—one papyrus refers to the legal public charges—suitable, or fit, genuine (true—genuine—yoke-fellow at Philippians 4:3). So "it becomes an epithet of affectionate appreciation (as in) II Timothy 1:2".[1] It is just as though Timothy and Titus had become the legal heirs, the sons of Paul—not just for material possessions but rather the sharers and inheritors of his spiritual wealth.

I TIMOTHY

We come then to Paul's first letter to Timothy, and at verse 1 of chapter 2 Paul urges that "first of all, supplication, prayers, *intercessions*, and giving of thanks, be made for all men".

A Petition From Twin Sisters

The word for "intercessions" is *enteuxeis*, and it has the idea of approaching a king and addressing a petition to him. This is the word used in a papyrus petition dating to 163 B.C.,[2] addressed to King Ptolemy and Queen Cleopatra. Twin sisters were in attendance at a heathen temple, and they were entitled to an allowance of oil and bread which had been withheld. So they petitioned for a restitution of their rights. It seems they had already successfully appealed on a previous occasion, but when their superiors departed, lesser officials ignored the judgment given in favour of the two girls. But they persisted, and as a result of their perseverance the case was investigated.

They used this word *enteuxeis* as they petitioned the royal couple. "We are wasting away through starvation," they claimed. "When we petitioned before, the impression was conveyed as if everything fitting would be done for us in good order, but for the remainder of the time this was not carried out." The story had a happy ending, for their petition was granted and they recovered most of what was due to them.

This petition also uses the word *parousia*, referring

to the royal appearance as their majesties visited the Egyptian city of Memphis.*

The petition from these twin sisters is quite long, and one of their points is that an official made all sorts of promises but then "*took no* further *account of* the matter". Here the twins use a similar expression to that in Acts 20:24: "*Of no account do I regard* my life," said Paul. The expression is a common one, as indeed are various other words used in this letter, such as that for "defrauding", reminding us of Mark 10:19—"*Defraud* not"—and I Corinthians 6:8—"Ye do wrong and *defraud* your brother."

About Bishops And Elders

Another notable word in the Pastoral Epistles is that for "bishop". It is not so long since it was wrongly argued that this word *episkopos* was not a first-century word, and could not have been used by Paul in the Pastoral Epistles, as at I Timothy 3:1: "This is a true saying, If a man desire the office of a *bishop*, he desireth a good work." Now this word has been found in the papyri, and its Hebrew equivalent *mebaqqer* occurs in the writings of the Dead Sea Scroll community found at Qumran. The English equivalent which has come to us from the Latin is supervisor. The Greek *episkopos* literally means *over- (epi-) seer (skopos)*—overseer.

Another word on which we have light is used by Paul at I Timothy 5:1—"Rebuke not an elder, but intreat him as a father" urges the Apostle, as he lays down instructions to be followed in the early Church. The word for "elder" is another Greek word, *presbuteros*, and this was used in Egypt as an honorific title relating to village or community officers. One example is that corn had to be collected in connection with the visit (*parousia*) of the king, and that this collection was to be made by the village principals.[3] The word is used in a similar way in other papyri. The word came to have a technical meaning, referring to the city elders, and was common in

*See chapter 6.

Graeco-Roman civic life. Elsewhere we refer to a priest who was charged with letting his hair grow too long (cf. I Corinthians 11:14), and the enquiry into this matter was carried out by the five presbyters—the priests. Here the word was used in relation to the priests of a pagan temple. In a petition dating to 117 B.C. a farmer is seeking protection of a high official. He asks the official to notify the fact of this protection to the village elders—the *presbuteroi*.

In the early Church the word was used in a rather similar technical sense relating to the elders of the Church.[4]

The same word is used elsewhere, including I Peter 5:1. There the elder is also the shepherd of the flock, and we find that he is to take the oversight of the flock "not for filthy lucre's sake". In our companion volume *New Light On The Gospels*, chapter 10, we saw that shepherds had a special interest to ensure the safe keeping of all their sheep because of their financial obligations in the event of a sheep being lost. In their case it was necessary to "take the oversight for filthy lucre's sake". The Christian elder, undershepherd to the Good Shepherd, was to love the sheep because they belonged to the Good Shepherd, the One Who had given His own life for the sheep.

As we go on through this First Epistle to Timothy we find listed the qualifications of the bishop. Among other things, he is to rule his own household well: "For if a man know not how to rule his own house, how shall he take care of the church of God?" (I Timothy 3:5).

This word "take care of" also appears in a very interesting papyrus document dating to 1 B.C. A soldier named Hilarion, away from home, is writing to his wife urging her "to take care of" their young child. He also writes about another child soon to be born: "If it is a male let it be, if a female expose it."[5]

This is written in the same decade as Herod's decree to slay all the babies born in Bethlehem, and it exhibits the same ruthless and callous spirit. Hilarion goes on to tell his wife that he cannot forget her, and he entreats her not to worry. But how could this prospective mother not worry when she had over her head the fear that her child might be a girl, and if so that it was to be destroyed? Sadly, this practice was all too common.

"Take Care"—The Christian Application

A letter known as "The Epistle of Diognetus", about 150 years later, makes it clear that Christians did not expose their children. Though the Christian writings were products of their times, they led men and women to higher ground, to standards that were greatly superior to those of the Greek and Roman worlds from which that literature emanated. They followed the teachings of Him Who said, "Suffer the little children to come unto Me, and forbid them not: for of such is the kingdom of God" (Mark 10:14).

The expression "take care of" in Hilarion's letter is the same as in the parable of the Good Samaritan, where we read that the Samaritan bound up the wounded man's injuries, brought him to the inn, and asked the innkeeper to "take care of him".

The spirit of Hilarion, whose interest in "taking care" of his offspring was so inconsistent, rather reminds us of Judas Iscariot, who should have been anxious for the welfare of his new spiritual brothers, but we read that he was a thief and "did not care"—the same root word —for the poor. It is worth mentioning in passing that another word used in this verse referring to Judas Iscariot (John 12:6) has light thrown on it from the papyrus. We refer to the word "bag"—*glōssokomon*. The original meaning of this word was "receptacle for the 'tongues' or mouthpieces of flutes".[6] This was a decidedly vernacular word which came to mean casket or box. The box was a portable one, but it was not a "bag" as we would think of it today. The Revised Version reading of "money-box" in this verse is much nearer the mark.

Other words in this same papyrus from Hilarion also remind us of New Testament usage, such as the employment of two different words *erōtaō* and *parakalō* for "beg" or "beseech". Both these words are used at I Thessalonians 4:1: "Furthermore then we beseech (*erōtaō*) you, brethren, and exhort (*parakalō*) you by the Lord Jesus . . ."

Yet another word is *opsōnia* which Hilarion uses to refer to his wages, and the same word is at Luke 3:14: "What shall we do?" the soldiers demanded of John the Baptist. "And he said unto them, Do violence to no man, neither accuse any falsely; and be content with your *wages*."

The Apostle Paul uses the word also at I Corinthians 9:7: "Who goeth to warfare any time at his own *charges*?" he asks.

The Term "Deacon"

Another church office to which Paul refers is that of "deacon" (*diakonos*—Timothy 3:8). The word simply means "servant", but we now know that this had gained a technical meaning before New Testament times. In the 1st century B.C. the holders of various offices associated with the dedication of a statue to the god Hermes include "deacons".[7] Another list of temple officials dating to about 100 B.C. concludes with "deacons". We even read of a "college" of deacons in the service of gods such as Serapis and Isis. Yet another "everyday" document, dating to A.D. 5, is a receipt for wheat which has been delivered by Ammonius the deacon.[8]

There are of course other words on which the papyrus throws light—words such as that at I Timothy 4:7 where the young man is urged to *exercise* himself unto godliness. The word is *gumnazō* and was popular in Paul's day. One writer tells that he had "a good bout with" certain others. At other times it has a general idea of someone who is "practising".[9] The one who would be concerned with holiness should be as determined to be spiritually fit as the athlete or the boxer is in the physical realm. In the very next verse a noun form of the word is used—"For bodily exercise profiteth for a little." It is not that bodily exercise is *not* profitable, but that spiritual exercise is that which must be practised by the

Christian. Paul is saying that the participant in athletic games strove for glory in this life, but the one who is spiritually fit is working towards the far higher goal of eternal values and the glorious life beyond death.

Another word from Paul's day is that for "silly women" (*gunakaria*) at II Timothy 3:6. We find from ancient writings that their male counterparts were specially identified by their neat, fashionably trimmed beard. The women regarded themselves as society ladies and they were known for their caprice and idle curiosity.[10]

II TIMOTHY

Not only do these papyrus documents show that words supposedly used only in the Bible were in common use after all; not only do they demonstrate how other words have been taken and ennobled with a new spiritual meaning: they also bring to life the everyday occupations of the class of people with whom the New Testament is so specially concerned. The papyrus documents have recovered for us "the forgotten multitudes" of the so-called lower classes—that great company of people who are virtually ignored in the classical Greek writings.

In New Testament and papyri alike we meet these people. We watch them at the market and in the home, paying their taxes, catching their fish, growing their crops, tending their sick. And again these significant activities remind us that our New Testament documents were the products of a particular culture—that of the Romans, who dominated Palestine in the time of Christ.

Let us briefly illustrate some of these "everyday" affairs from Paul's second letter to Timothy, and also from Titus.

The pathos of II Timothy—Paul's last letter—as the aged Apostle urges Timothy to come to him in his need is somewhat paralleled by a letter from Paniskos to Ploutogenia: "So when you have received this letter of mine make your necessary preparations to come quickly if I send for you."[11]

88

"Just Like Your Mother"

Later on Paniskos writes again to his wife, complaining that she has not been obedient. In fact, she was acting remarkably like his mother-in-law: "I know your mother does this!" Paniskos grumbles.

As he goes on he reminds us of Paul's description in Ephesians 6 of the Christian's armour: "Send me my helmet and my shield, and my five lances and my breastplate and my belt."

In another letter—for Paniskos was a ready writer—he asks his wife to make ready his cloak with a hood, and our mind goes to Paul's request to Timothy to bring him the cloak he left at Troas. A similar message comes in a letter, now in the Berlin Museum, which Mnesiergus wrote to his household: "Mnesiergus sendeth to them that are at his house greeting and health and he saith it is so with him. If ye be willing, send me some covering, either sheepskins or goatskins."

"He Oft Refreshed Me"

Another interesting word is "refreshed"—"Onesiphorus oft *refreshed* me and he was not ashamed of my chain" we read at II Timothy 1:16. The word "refreshed" (*anapsuchō*) is in a letter from Isias to her husband.[12] She is in what she calls "the last extremity" because of the high price of corn. She had expected her husband to return before this, and she hoped for some *relief*.

Anapsuchō contains the root of *psuchē*, "soul", and embraces also the idea of the refreshing being in the area of the soul. It is used at Acts 3:19 where we read, "Repent ye therefore, and be converted, that your sins may be blotted out, when the times of *refreshing* shall come from the presence of the Lord." After sins have been blotted out, times of refreshing come: Isias hoped for refreshment when her husband came, and hoped that her great privation would be for ever past. The Christian knows that his dire extremity *is* past, for the times of refreshing have come from the Lord, and our sins are already forgiven.

Extracts From Timothy On Papyrus

Often these old papyrus letters quote from New Testament documents. Thus a man named Paieous, writing to someone for whom he has great respect, tells of his joy because of that person's faith and love towards everyone.[13] He is glad because of his friend's manner of life, and goes on to refer to his concern as a soldier of Christ. Then he quotes loosely from II Timothy 2:4—"No one that is a soldier mixes himself in the affairs of this life." He rejoices because of his father's uprightness and comments: "For the scripture saith, Whosoever believeth on Him shall not be put to shame." Clearly the Scriptures were precious to these saints of God, living some three hundred years after the verses they quoted had been used by the New Testament writers.

In these letters Scripture after Scripture is quoted—we read such expressions as "redeeming the time because the days are evil",[14] and the same papyrus stresses that Dorotheus (a man) hopes to meet his friend "if the Lord will." These people were still living in the simplicity of faith expected by the New Testament writers.

TITUS

We move on, briefly, to Titus.

The Royal Proclamation "Entrusted" To Titus

At Titus 1:3 Paul tells Titus that he has been entrusted with the proclamation of the gospel by the commandment of God our Saviour. Actually Paul uses this expression "I am entrusted with" several times—at Galatians 2:7, I Corinthians 9:17, I Thessalonians 2:4, and I Timothy 1:11.

This is paralleled in Greek documents where the emperor has a secretary who is "entrusted with" the writing of certain letters—like Titus, the secretary was *entrusted with* certain royal proclamations.

The figure is taken further at II Corinthians 3:3 where Paul actually refers to the people themselves as being a letter of Christ—"ministered by us." He goes on to say that this is a letter not written with ink, "Forasmuch as ye are manifestly declared to be the epistle of Christ ministered by us, written not with ink, but with the Spirit of the living God: not in tables of stone, but in the fleshy tables of the heart." A major aspect of this teaching is that other people can read them, and see something of the character of Christ in them. Paul is the agent, the "secretary", and he writes on behalf of Christ his Lord —he is entrusted with the gospel and so he writes about it.

In somewhat similar fashion the seven letters to the churches in the Revelation also have been illuminated. They remind us of the many imperial letters written to corporations and cities, published as inscriptions, and so available for reading by all.

"To The Pure . . ."

At Titus 1:15 we read, "Unto the pure all things are pure: but unto them that are defiled and unbelieving is nothing pure; but even their mind and conscience is defiled." Two of these words are in the report of a dream dating to 160 B.C.: "If these women are defiled," we read at the conclusion of the dream, "They shall never again be pure."[15]

Again illustrating the "everyday language" of our New Testament documents, we find that this papyrus uses various other words common to both the New Testament and the papyri—words such as "mercy" in the expression to the gods, "Show thyself merciful." "Have pity," these gods are invoked. The word for "street" is the same as at Matthew 6:2 concerning the trumpet being blown in the street, and Acts 9:11 where Ananias comes to the street where Paul was living, and Acts 12:10 which tells of Peter coming out into the street from prison. Simple, everyday words—yes, but these and ever so many others indicate that the New Testament records were written in the common idiom of those times.

"Let No Man Despise Thee"

Yet another word on which light is thrown is that for "despise" at Titus 2:15: "Let no man despise thee." The same word is on a papyrus document where a widow complains concerning two overseers who "despised my inability" and so mismanaged her affairs. The Christian in the will of God is God-appointed, and is capable of carrying out the work entrusted to him. As a royal ambassador he must let none despise him. This of course does not open the door to boastfulness or arrogance.

Qualities Of A Good Wife

An inscription from the tombstone of Aticulaea, who died at Pergamum about the time of the Emperor Hadrian, reads, "Julius Bassus to Otacilia Polla, his sweetest wife. Loving to her husband, and loving to her children, she lived with him unblamably thirty years."

It is relevant to put this alongside Titus 2:4, 5 where Paul exhorts young women to be loving to their husbands —"to be discreet, chaste, keepers at home, good, obedient to their own husbands, that the Word of God be not blasphemed."

Ethical concepts are known on inscriptions, and in ancient lists of virtues and vices. Paul also lists vices at such places as I Corinthians 6:9, 10 and I Timothy 1:9, 10, and there are New Testament catalogues of virtues, at at II Peter 1:5, 6. Virtues as well as vices are listed in old records, as in the 1st century B.C. inscription in honour of Herostratus, the son of Dorcalion. His inventory included good qualities such as virtue, godliness and diligence.

At first sight it might seem that the New Testament writers have merely copied the ethical teachings of surrounding peoples. In the same way it sometimes appears that Old Testament writers have copied from *their* neighbours, but closer examination shows that the surface similarities do little more than demonstrate that these people wrote against the background claimed for them. Very often it is the differences, rather than the similarities, which show the consistent and marked superiority and uniqueness of the Bible writings.

These then are some of the ways in which the papyrus throws light on the Epistles of Paul. The spirit of the papyrus letters is often similar to the New Testament Epistles, and we are frequently reminded that the New Testament is overflowing with the language of ordinary people. The New Testament writers such as Paul are not especially thinking in terms of posterity—they are uninhibited, with little thought that one day their every word will be weighed, examined, debated, becoming the source of joy and—sadly—of division. In the wisdom of God His method was to use the "everyday". And because of this the papyri and the ostraca have combined to declare authoritatively that these New Testament writings are genuine, the products of the times they claimed for themselves.

REFERENCES

[1]Moulton, J. H., and Milligan, G. *The Vocabulary Of The Greek Testament*, pp. 128f.
[2]Milligan, G. *Selections From The Greek Papyri*, pp. 12ff., P. Par. No. 26.
[3]Moulton, J. H., and Milligan, G. *Ibid.*, p. 535, P. Tebt. I.48, about 113 B.C.
[4]*Ibid.*, e.g. Oxy. Pap. No. VIII.1162.
[5]Milligan, G. *Ibid.*, pp. 32f., Oxy. Pap. No. 744.
[6]Moulton, J. H., and Milligan, G. *Ibid.*, p. 128.
[7]*Ibid.*, p. 149.
[8]*J.E.A.* XXIII (1937), p. 225.
[9, 10]Moulton, J. H., and Milligan, G. *Ibid.*, p. 133.
[11]*J.E.A.* XIII (1927), p. 62.
[12]Milligan, G. *Ibid.*, p. 8ff., P. Brit. Mus. 42, 168 B.C.
[13]Pap. No. 1921.
[14]Pap. No. 1927.
[15]P. Par. No. 51.

8

The "Title Deeds"—
And Other Illustrations

(*Hebrews, James, I and II Peter, Jude*)

Introduction
What a wide range of writings we have in this section
following Paul's letters! How would these matters have
been dealt with in modern times? The Epistle of James
is "to the twelve tribes scattered abroad"—would he
reach them by a radio broadcast today—or a television
programme—instead of by a personal letter? Would
John have telephoned his friend Gaius instead of writing
his Third Epistle? Would he have sketched his visions
on to off-set printing plates in sending the Revelation
to the seven churches?

But perhaps it is all best just as it is after all! As we
turn briefly to each of these Books we find that the
papyrus and other archaeological evidence assure us that
they are indeed products of New Testament times. Space
allows us to select only a few illustrations from the
many available.

In this first of two chapters we glance quickly at
Hebrews, James, I and II Peter, and Jude.

HEBREWS
We do not know the human author of the Epistle to the
Hebrews. Paul, Barnabas, Luke, Priscilla—these names
have been put forward as possibilities, but all we can
say with certainty is that finally the Author is the Holy
Spirit Himself—the Author of *all* Scripture.

It is sometimes argued that the differences in style
between the earlier documents of the Christian Church

94

and this Epistle to the Hebrews are explained by factors associated with development. For instance, by the time Hebrews was written Christianity was beginning to be accepted more widely as the true religion, and so there is a sense in which its documents were becoming more "literary". From the literary point of view, it is suggested, this was a new era, an advance beyond what some have called the "uninhibited writers" of the first decades after Christ's death and resurrection.

Today it is recognized that some views—first put forward in modern times by Adolf Deissmann—as to the "popular" nature of the New Testament writings were rather too sweeping.* It is true that the New Testament was written in the language of its times, and that it was *koine* Greek, the language of everyday people. However, it is widely agreed today that Dr. Deissmann went too far with his suggestion that the New Testament documents were not literary. Some of the writings are indeed in the nature of letters primarily intended for 1st century Christians, but other Epistles such as Romans, Ephesians, and Colossians are literary in the truest sense of the word. It is universally accepted that this is true of Hebrews.

The Search For The Messiah
At chapter 3 of our companion volume *New Light On The Gospels* we considered the evidence as the Jewish people searched for their Messiah. Yet when that Messiah was presented to them they rejected Him. We saw how the Dead Sea Scroll community collected Messianic prophecies, but could not reconcile their own Scriptures and so looked for more than one Messiah. How could one person be a King of the line of David, a Priest from the house of Levi, the Great Prophet like unto Moses, and a Priest with the rank of Melchisedec?

It is enlightening to study the Epistle to the Hebrews against the background of the times, and to realize that the unknown author of this Epistle was making it clear

*See *New Light On The Gospels*, chapter 1.

that Jesus was the Messiah. At chapter 1 he tells us that Jesus Christ is the Son of God (verses 2ff.); He is not only greater than man, but He is also superior to angels (verses 4ff.); He is the King of Kings (verses 8ff.), and at the same time He is our effective High Priest (verse 3—see also 7:24ff. etc.)

At Hebrews 3 we learn that Jesus Christ is greater than Moses, the great prophet of Israel, while chapter 4 tells us that He is a greater Leader than their military commander, Joshua. He is also greater than Abraham, for Abraham paid tithes to Melchisedec who was a type of the Lord Jesus Christ, the eternal High Priest. (Tithes were paid only to a superior.)

The Dead Sea Scrolls And Melchisedec
A number of Dead Sea Scroll fragments from Cave No. 11 at Qumran referred to Melchisedec. In these Melchisedec was linked with a series of Old Testament quotations. He was associated with divine judgment, and also with Isaiah 52:7 which reads: "How beautiful upon the mountains are the feet of him that bringeth good tidings, that published peace; that bringeth good tidings of good, that publisheth salvation; that saith unto Zion, Thy God reigneth!" Thus Melchisedec was linked with both the favour of God, and with the judgment of God. He could call alongside him the angelic spirits of heaven.

The writer of this text concerning Melchisedec certainly saw him as one who exercises divine prerogatives. And though the Epistle to the Hebrews is not presenting the same picture as that of the Qumran text, there is at least a measure of similarity. It becomes clear that Jewish thinking about Melchisedec was to identify him in some way with the promised deliverance, with release and salvation.

Possibly Jewish thought identified him with Michael the Archangel—for Jewish tradition looked on Melchisedec as High Priest, and Michael is called the Heavenly High Priest in the Babylonian Talmud.

Though the Qumran fragments have no influence on the New Testament text—for the comments in Hebrews are based on the two Old Testament references as such —yet there is a measure of similarity in these two "Jewish" writings, for each exalts Melchisedec as a heavenly redemption figure. But the New Testament application to Jesus Christ is clear, giving a picture of Him Who has no beginning of days. It recognizes that He is *not* of the line of Levi (Hebrews 7:13-22), for His is an eternal priesthood. In the Epistle to the Hebrews the strands come together as we are given a perfect picture of the eternal High Priest with the rank of Melchisedec.

Light From The Papyri
Let us consider two representative words in Hebrews on which the papyri have thrown light.

One word common in New Testament times is *koinōnos*, used for instance in a letter which a father writes telling his son that he must return to assume his responsibilities on the farm. "Our *partner* has taken no share in the work," he wrote. "Not only was the well not cleaned out, but also the water channel was choked with sand, and the whole land is untilled."

The word for "partner" in this letter is *koinōnos*, and this is the word we have at Hebrews 10:33—"You became *companions* (partners) of them that were so used." In similar fashion we read of James and John who were "partners" with Simon Peter (Luke 5:10).

This partnership is somewhat similar to what we find with two men from Egypt, Hermes and Cornelius,[1] though Cornelius takes over only a sixth share in the rent of a lake of which Hermes had a lease.

FAITH—The "Title-Deeds"
Another well-known Bible verse illustrated from the papyri is Hebrews 11:1: "Now faith is the *substance* of things hoped for, the evidence of things not seen." The Greek word used here for "substance" is *hupostasis*, and it is used in the "Petition of Dionysia," a widow who makes a property claim to the Prefect of Egypt. This petition is part of a collection of papers bearing on the

97

possession of the property, and this word has a meaning similar to our modern "title-deeds."

The word is used in a number of other papyri—one fragment is translated "More *land* than I actually possess",[2] the word "land" there being *hupostasis*. Yet another reads, "and out of this *estate* I declare that my husband owes me . . ,"[3] *hupostasis* there being translated as "estate". Various papyri make it clear that the word involves the idea of a written undertaking as regards property. The word distinctly relates to the documents which bear on the ownership of property, such documents having been properly drawn up and deposited with the legal authorities: they have become the basis of evidence of ownership.

A helpful comment comes from Drs. Moulton and Milligan:

> "These varied uses are at first sight somewhat perplexing, but in all cases there is the same central idea of something that *underlies* visible conditions and guarantees a future possession. And as this is the essential meaning in Hebrews 11:1, we venture to suggest the translation 'Faith is the *title-deed* of things hoped for.' "[4]

Thus in this verse we are reminded that though we cannot physically or materially handle all our spiritual possessions, they are guaranteed by faith—faith is the "title-deed".

We take God at His word—that is faith. It is as though He has put His signature to our spiritual inheritance rights, and though we cannot *see* our inheritance, by faith we claim it. The title-deeds are ours!

With all the new light and new knowledge of this wonderful twentieth century, yet an Epistle such as that to the Hebrews is still as accepted as ever it was. The "new light" has not shown us who the author is, but has accentuated the genuineness of the document.

THE GENERAL EPISTLES

We come to the Epistles of James and Peter. These are often referred to as "catholic" or "general" Epistles, the others being I, II and III John, and Jude. This title was given to distinguish them from the Pauline Epistles and that to the Hebrews.

JAMES

James is addressed to the twelve tribes scattered abroad (chapter 1:1), and so is especially relevant to churches composed of Christian Jews. James would have met many of those he addressed, for Jews from all nations visited Jerusalem at the time of the Passover (see Acts 2:5). No doubt he recognized the tendency to earthly gain which typified many of them after their conversion, and there is much practical wisdom on such matters as the right use of wealth in this letter. Indeed, this Epistle is a "wisdom" writing—along the lines of Old Testament Books such as Job, Psalms and Proverbs. It is quite definitely superior to the so-called "Apocryphon of James",* a writing containing gnostic elements, and a typical Jewish Apocryphal document that was not considered worthy of a place in the Canon of Scripture.

Another piece of practical advice—"wisdom" writing—in James relates to the taking of oaths. It is little wonder that James wrote, "Swear not at all," (chapter 5:12) for in all sorts of insignificant matters the swearing of an oath was by the emperor. There are many illustrations of this from the papyrus documents dating to the very generation of James, such as this one: "I swear by Nero Claudius Caesar Augustus Germanicus Imperator that I have levied no contributions for any purpose whatever in the said village."[5]

It is also true that Jewish people had developed the tradition of swearing oaths very lightly. James' admonition was not directed primarily at judicial oaths, for these were acceptable according to Old Testament law (Jeremiah 12:16; 42:5). Rather he was attacking the wrong use of this sacred practice—wrong as regards the true God and wrong when taken in the name of false deities such as the emperor.

*See *New Light On The Gospels*, chapter 5.

The Sincere Milk Of The Word

One of the most interesting words on which the papyri have thrown light is at I Peter 2:2 where we have the injunction, "As newborn babes, desire the *sincere* milk of the word, that ye may grow thereby."

This word *adolos*—"sincere" in the Authorized Version, or "spiritual" as it is in the Revised Version—actually means "unadulterated". It is used in ancient writings to refer to something that is not mixed with anything else. Thus one scrap of papyrus refers to "new wheat, pure and *unadulterated*, not mixed with barley".

In another papyrus,[6] dating to A.D. 188, objection is made to the fact that two ship-loads of wheat had been examined and they proved to be *adulterated* with barley and earth. The officer-in-charge is told to collect the deficiency from the owner, together with a penalty. In this particular case the wheat was "under measure by 2 per cent of barley and likewise ½ per cent of earth".

When we apply this word specifically to the verse in I Peter we learn that we are being urged to desire the full acceptance of the teachings of the Word of God itself—not "mixed" with "outside" ideas. The implication is that we do not go even to such sources as Church history or to Inter-Testamental practices for our "Thus saith the Lord", but we come to the Word of God itself. In its pages we will find the principles whereby the guidance of God can be known to us.

If only we would obey this injunction many problems would be resolved, for it is undoubtedly confusing to attempt to find the will of God through the history of the Church. The Scriptural position is that the Word of God takes precedence over the dictate of any church on earth. Church history is a shaky reed on which to lean, for so often interpretations of events throughout history have led men to opposite conclusions.

Elsewhere the Apostle Paul writes, "Now we have received, not the spirit of the world, but the spirit which is of God; that we might know the things that are freely given to us of God. Which things also we speak, not in the words which man's wisdom teacheth, but which the Holy Ghost teacheth; comparing spiritual things with spiritual" (I Corinthians 2:12, 13).

We are to take note of "the words ... which the Holy Ghost teacheth". If we really want to know the mind of God we will do well to follow the example of those Berean Christians who "searched the Scriptures daily" (Acts 17:11).

Fellow-Heirs
Another word now better understood is at I Peter 3:7 where we read of the wife being spiritually *fellow-heir* with her husband. This was another word supposedly unknown outside the Bible, but it now has been found in an Ephesian inscription of the New Testament era, where a man named Umphuleius Bassus refers to "Eutychis as co-heir".

The Title "Chief Shepherd"
Enlightenment also comes as to the injunction to be "ensamples to the flock. And when the Chief Shepherd shall appear, ye shall receive a crown of glory that fadeth not away" (I Peter 5:3ff.). The title "Chief Shepherd" was not invented for Biblical purposes—as previously thought—but was borrowed from the culture of the times. A piece of wood was found hanging around the neck of an Egyptian mummy, dating to New Testament times, and the inscription read: "Plenis the Younger, Chief Shepherd." The genitive case is wrongly used and the inscription is actually "chief shepherd's"—it is probable that this was a slip in writing. It is believed that this was a title given to a man who had other shepherds under him—and incidentally it is yet another reminder of the many titles correctly used right through the Scriptures.

II PETER
It would require another volume to develop the concept of past, present, and future in II Peter. He accepts the

actuality of the Flood (II Peter 3:6), and of the destruction of Sodom and Gomorrah (chapter 2:6ff.). Thus he accepts the Scriptures as they relate to the past. As to the present and his own age, he tells us that "we have not followed cunningly devised fables" and goes on to say "we were eye-witnesses of His majesty" (II Peter 1:16, 17). He has a continuing experience of the risen Christ, the One to Whom he referred as "the Rock" (*Petra*) (I Peter 2:8).

As to the future, he believes in the coming of the day of the Lord (II Peter 3:12), and in doing so makes amazing statements such as that relating to the elements melting with intense heat (verse 10). This is much better understood now that we have seen a precursor of this event: for in this age of the atomic bomb we know a little of what is meant by the expression, "the elements shall melt with fervent heat."

Living In The Light Of Heaven

In this context Peter challenges Christian men and women, "Seeing then that all these things shall be dissolved, what manner of persons ought ye to be in all holy *conversation* and godliness." This word "conversation" is *anastrophē* (see also Galatians 1:13; Ephesians 2:3; and I Peter 1:15).

It refers to much more than spoken words, but rather to behaviour, or way of life. Indeed, it involves the concept of a complete turn around, a reversal. It can mean "to turn up and down", and it came to imply behaviour that was open for all to see. Such exemplary conduct is referred to in papyri and on inscriptions. In the Christian's walk his behaviour should become radically different from what it was before conversion to Jesus Christ. He is as a book that all men can see and read, rather reminding us of the statement about Peter himself and John: ". . . they took knowledge of them, that they had been with Jesus" (Acts 4:13).

JUDE

It is interesting to find that Jude refers to Jewish apocryphal literature—for example, verse 9 is found in "The

Assumption of Moses", while verse 14 seems to be a loose quotation from the Book of Enoch—"Behold, the Lord cometh with ten thousands of his saints . . ."

Quoting From Enoch

It is sometimes a problem to Bible students that Jude is quoting from this Inter-Testamental Book as though it was written in the times of Enoch. However, though it is true that the Book was compiled not long before the time of Christ on earth, it is also true that it is a composition from various authors. It is by no means impossible that part of it could have come originally from Enoch.

The second problem sometimes raised is that Jude is thus endorsing the Book of Enoch as genuine in all its parts, but this is not a valid argument. The Apostle Paul quotes three Greek poets—from Aratus of Soli, at Acts 17:28, from Menander (I Corinthians 15:33), and from Epimenides (Titus 1:12). This does not mean that Paul endorsed all that these poets wrote. And similarly Jude is simply quoting a passage from a non-canonical book, and we accept this particular prediction as from God. This quotation from Enoch is inspired because it has been included in the sacred Canon, but no such seal is on the rest of the Book of Enoch.

Jude was probably using a current idea to teach a spiritual lesson, and the Holy Spirit has seen fit to include this particular statement in Holy Writ. The Holy Spirit of God has used many literary forms and devices, and in them all we are able to say, "*All* Scripture is given by inspiration of God."

We saw that our spiritual possessions are guaranteed by faith—that faith is the title-deed. And as we continue to study the light thrown on New Testament documents we are assured that our faith is indeed reasonable. For these human documents also have stamped upon them the imprint of the finger of God.

REFERENCES

[1]Pap. Amh. 100.

[2]Oxy. Pap. No. III.488.
[3]Oxy. Pap. No. X.1274.
[4]Moulton, J. H., and Milligan, G. *The Vocabulary Of The Greek Testament*, p. 660.
[5]Oxy. Pap. No. 239, A.D. 66.
[6]Oxy. Pap. No. 708, A.D. 188.

9

Letters From John

(I, II, and III John, and Revelation)

In this chapter we look briefly at the letters John wrote
—three Epistles and the Revelation. For after all was not
the Revelation also a letter to the churches? And not
only churches of Asia, but churches of Europe and elsewhere too. For the message of the Revelation is still
relevant today.

THE EPISTLES OF JOHN
When we come to the Epistles of John, we are reminded
of the similarity to John's Gospel. The Apostle talks of
such concepts as life, love, light, darkness and truth.
These expressions are also used by the Dead Sea Scroll
community, as in "The War of the Sons of Light and the
Sons of Darkness". Formerly it was claimed that John's
Gospel and his Epistles were Hellenistic in outlook and
not Jewish, but since the finding of the Dead Sea Scrolls
in 1947 and the succeeding years, all that has changed.
It is now recognized that John was indeed using the
language of his own people, against the background of
his own times. "Brotherly Love", "Fountain of Living
Water", "Truth and Perversity"—these and other expressions are common to John and the Dead Sea Scrolls.

I JOHN
It is sometimes conjectured that John's First Epistle was
especially for the churches in Asia, perhaps the very ones
mentioned in the first three chapters of Revelation. The
writer knows those who are addressed, and calls them
"little children". If John spent his last years in Ephesus,

as seems probable, it is likely he would indeed know many to whom he was writing.

His special interest was to meet the doctrinal and practical needs of his readers, among many of whom he himself had laboured (I John 2:7, 12–14, 20–27). In this Epistle he majors on points of knowledge, well-illustrated by the last three verses—"We know that we are of God . . . We know that the Son of God is come . . . We know Him that is true."

True knowledge is through the Lord Jesus Christ, and is not vested in the heretical gnosticism which had already intruded into the churches. The recovered papyri have shown how necessary and urgent it was that gnostic and other heresies should be refuted.

So John denounced deceivers and anti-Christs (2:22, 4:15, 5:1). These latter were probably the Ebionites (Judaizers) and the followers of Cerinthus who denied the Deity of Christ, teaching that Christ was only human, a mere man. John challenged the Docetites who claimed that Christ had no real body, and so only appeared to suffer. He addressed himself to this view as he declared that Christ is come in the flesh (chapter 4:1, 2). He also denounced those who denied the true humanity of Christ (1:1, 4:3, 5:6). He insisted that Christ was Man, and just as surely that He was also God.

John also insisted on purity of worship and service, saying that every sin is a transgression (3:4) and that fellowship with God will lead to purity (2:5, 3:8–10, 4:13, 5:11). This was in direct contrast to the teachings of some gnostics who denied responsibility for sins committed in the body, the argument being that matter is evil and they were simply unfortunate in being imprisoned in a body of flesh.*

Saviour Of The World
John also ennobled concepts already known, showing that Christ was the true Life, the Light of the World,

*See *New Light On The Gospels*, chapter 4, and also chapter 4 in this volume.

and the very manifestation of the God of Love. Another concept to which he gave a higher spiritual meaning than in its secular use was that of "Saviour of the World"—*sōtēr tou kosmou* (see I John 4:14, also John 4:42). This title was well-known, being ascribed to various Roman emperors, including Julius Caesar, Augustus, Claudius, Vespasian and Titus.

Against that background it is enlightening to read I John 4:14 "And we have seen and do testify that the Father sent the Son to be *the Saviour of the World*."

Those Roman emperors could not bring true salvation to the world, and the moral depravity of the Roman era is well-attested. But in the fulness of time God sent His Son, the true Saviour of the World. A new dynamic was needed, and spiritual power was given through Him Who came to conquer sin, and death, and hell.

The Caesars opposed Christianity and sought to stamp it out as a hated and despised Jewish heresy. Their representative agreed to the crucifixion of the Founder of Christianity, and in other ways they sought to nullify this new influence sweeping the world. Thus thousands of disciples died rather than offer a pinch of incense to the Caesar as a god. But those martyrs lived on in the presence of the true Saviour of the World. Had He not already declared, "My Kingdom is not of this world?" (John 18:36).

II AND III JOHN

Scholars through the years have debated the meaning of the term *kuria* which John uses at the opening of his Second Epistle—"The elder unto the elect *lady*," and again at verse 5 we read, "Now I beseech thee *lady*"— in both these verses *kuria* is translated as "lady". Some have thought that *kuria* was a proper name, the actual name of the lady addressed. Others have suggested it was a way of referring to a sister church; others again have interpreted it simply to mean "lady", for this is a Greek word for "lady".

The papyrus has resolved the problem, as in one letter dating to the late 1st century.[1] In this document Indike writes to "Thaisous the lady", and here is the word *kuria*. This is just a simple note in which Indike is asking if the lady has received the bread basket sent by Taurinus the camel man. Other papyrus letters use *kuria* in the same way: such as a letter dating to 17 June, 1 B.C. In this an Egyptian workman named Hilarion is writing to his wife, and after greeting her he also sends greetings to "Beris my *lady*". In this letter it is simply a courteous form of address, as it is in John's Second Epistle.

"I Rejoiced Greatly"

This same letter from Hilarion has a similar expression to that found at both II John verse 4, and III John verse 3. "When I knew that you were doing well," this soldier writes to his sister, "*I rejoiced greatly*." The Apostle John uses this same expression as he says, "*I rejoiced greatly* that I found your children walking in truth" (II John verse 4), and then he writes to Gaius (in the 3rd Epistle) and says, "*I rejoiced greatly* when the brethren came and bore witness of the truth, even that you walk in truth."

At III John verse 14 the aged Apostle asks that his friends be greeted by name, and we have seen that this is paralleled in various papyri. One letter is from Irenaeus to his brother Apolinarius, and he uses language which reminds us strongly of John's Epistles. After a brief message as to his safe arrival, he writes: "I greet your wife much, and Serenus, and all who love you by name." This is similar to what the Apostle says at III John verse 14—"Our friends salute thee. Greet the friends by name."

The following papyrus letter is so similar in some points to John's third letter that we could almost imagine that this also was written by the beloved Apostle:

> "Heliodorus to Epidorus, greeting. If you are in health and all else goes as you wish, it is well: I, too, am getting on pretty well. I have written to you before in order to have a talk with you before I sail down, and now, if you see fit, I shall be obliged if you will meet me, preferably on the 20th . . . (Addressed) To Epidorus, sitologus."[2]

THE REVELATION

It might seem strange to include Revelation under a title *New Light on New Testament Letters*, but this writing was to be delivered to the churches, seven of which are mentioned in the first three chapters of this Book.

Why Apocalyptic Writings?

Revelation was written in a time of persecution when infant Christianity was faced with extreme opposition from civil powers, as well as with heresies and corruptions within. Among other purposes, John was inspired to write in order to meet these conditions, and to assure Christian people that Christ and His gospel must prevail. The literary method of the Apocalypse was well-known to the Jews, for Apocalyptic writings were used to stimulate the people in times of national crises, with the assurance that God's deliverer would be raised up. By the Apocalyptic method, symbolic pictures were used to present spiritual truths, and to show how Divine intervention could be forthcoming.

As to the importance of this Book in Scripture, the following outline by Dr. Clarence Benson is relevant:

> "Centering Christ as the foundation and fundamental of all Scripture, the contents of the entire Bible can be compressed into four lines:
>> Old Testament—The King and Saviour prophesied
>> Gospels—The King rejected; the Saviour revealed
>> Acts, Epistles—The Saviour proclaimed; the King concealed
>> Revelation—The King and Saviour glorified!"

Dr. Benson further writes:

> "The Gospels, the Acts and the Epistles abound with many quotations from the Old Testament, but the Revelation has more quotations than any other New Testament Book. In Matthew there are 92 such quotations, in Hebrews 102, but in Revelation 285 such references."[3]

The following is but a brief selection of some of the

ways in which the papyrus has thrown light on this wonderful concluding chapter of the Book of Scripture.

Written Within And Without...

We now have a better idea of the comment which we read at Revelation 5:1 as to a book written within, and without, and on the front, and on the back, and sealed with seven seals. It was not the usual practice to write on both sides of papyrus, but there are several known cases where both sides were used, and this explains the reference to the book being written on both sides.

"Sealed with seven seals" means that it was completely sealed. Documents were thoroughly sealed, and when this was at the direction of a high official no one dared break that seal without proper authority. One example of this relates to a deed that was sealed, and it was not to be opened until the appointed time before a proper court of law. This was a guarantee against forgery.

Only the Lion of the Tribe of Judah could break the seals of that book referred to at Revelation 5: this was no forgery, nor was the time premature. He prevailed, and the Divine purposes were accomplished.

In the next chapter (Revelation 6) we watch as six of the seals are opened, and as the fifth of these was undone John told of seeing "the souls of them that were slain for the word of God, and for the testimony which they held" (verse 9). Thousands died for the testimony of Jesus, and we who live in relative freedom easily forget that as the Apostle Paul and other 1st century Christians refused to recognize any but Jesus Christ as God, they were taking their lives in their hands. Those who would not make the usual sacrifices to the gods, including the Caesar, were often ruthlessly destroyed. They were forced to make a declaration such as the following:

> "It has always been my custom to sacrifice to the gods, and now in your presence in accordance with the decrees I have sacrificed and poured libations and tasted the offerings, and I request you to counter-sign my statement."[4]

The Christian could not make such a declaration, and

the history of the martyrs is clear indication that men were prepared to die rather than renounce the Divine Son of God. We today may not be called upon to die, but let us as true soldiers of Christ be prepared to go forth with our Lord outside the camp, bearing His reproach (Hebrews 13:13).

"Accuser Of The Brethren"

In Revelation 12:10 we read of the "accuser of the brethren". The picture is of the saints rejoicing because their accuser is cast down, the one who had accused the believers before God day and night. The Greek word is *katēgōr* and again this word was reckoned to be basic-ally a Bible word. One of the magical papyri translated by the late Sir Frederic Kenyon has this expression: "A charm to bind the senses, effective against everybody: for it works against enemies and *accusers* and robbers and terrors and dream-spectres." The word for accuser is not used to refer only to the devil, but also to human enemies; however, in a special sense the devil is "the accuser of the brethren".

Slaves

At Revelation 18:13 the word *sōmata* (bodies) has come to mean slaves. There the merchants of the earth are weeping, unable to make fortunes any more. A list of the things they have sold is given and this included *sōmata*, translated in the Authorized Version as slaves—a correct use, as is shown for us in a number of papyrus docu-ments. We read of "wages for the slaves",[5] of a slave being arrested,[6] unsold slaves included in a will.[7] One document warns, "Slaves are very dear here, and it is inexpedient to buy."[8]

"I Live Again..."

As we conclude, we briefly consider the word *anazaō* ("I live again"). This was regarded as a strictly Biblical word, especially as it seemed to go beyond the Greek ideas as to immortality of the soul. In days gone by scholars have put forward learned arguments to show why other Greek words did not convey the full sense demanded by *anazaō*.

However, this word has also appeared in Greek texts. One writer named Sotion refers to all sorts of marvels in the 1st century A.D., and among other things he tells of a body of water near Cilicia with supposed magical qualities. He says that strangled birds and other creatures will *come to life* if they are plunged in this water. The word used for "come to life" is the same as in the Scriptural usage.

Another example is concerning an interpreter of dreams named Artemidorus. In the 2nd century A.D. he wrote about the *return to life* of one who had been supposed dead, and again this "living again" is described by the word used at Revelation 20:5—"But the rest of the dead *lived not again* until the thousand years were finished. This is the first resurrection."

This word was known throughout the Greek-speaking world, and it has been given a new spiritual relevance because of the impact of Christianity.

REFERENCES

[1]Grenfell, B. P., and Hunt, A. S. *The Oxyrhynchus Papyri*, Part II, p. 301, Oxy. Pap. No. 300, dating late 1st century.
[2]Hunt, A. S., and Smyly, J. G. *The Tebtunis Papyri*, Volume III, Part I, p. 176.
[3]Benson, C. H. *A Guide For Bible Study*, pp. 79f.
[4]Milligan, G. *Selections From The Greek Papyri*, pp. 115f., B.G.U. 287, A.D. 50.
[5]P. Cairo Zen I.59027.
[6]P. Hib. I.54.
[7]Oxy. Pap. No. III.493.
[8]P. Ryl. II.244.

Conclusion

In this survey we have seen some of the ways in which the background of New Testament times has come to life. It has become ever clearer that writer after writer of the New Testament documents was thoroughly familiar with the setting against which he wrote. Insignificant points are referred to quite casually, without explanation, for the writers do not need to explain that which is already well-known to the recipients. The original New Testament records were contemporary with the events they described. They are first-class historical writings, preserved by meticulous copying in a way that is infinitely superior to other documents of the same period.

We have also seen that they bring to life the seemingly insignificant "lower classes" of Roman times, people overlooked—indeed, ignored—in extant secular records of that age.

Equally important is the new understanding of a large number of New Testament words, thought before this century to be known only in the Sacred Records, but now recognized as part of the living vocabulary of everyday people. They were used confidently by New Testament writers. They were often ennobled and given a new spiritual significance, but they undoubtedly belonged to New Testament times.

And yet these words live on, applicable not only to the 1st century A.D., but reaching just as effectively, down through the ages, into the 20th century. For as the Lord Jesus Christ said, "My words shall not pass away" (Mark 13:31). His words—and inspired words of His early disciples and Apostles—continue to be heard today, ringing with the same conviction as when they were first spoken and written nineteen hundred years ago. For these New Testament documents are part of God's revealed Word of Truth (John 17:17).

Bibliography

The books and journals consulted in the preparation of this volume include the following:

BOOKS

Allen, I. *The Early Church And The New Testament* (London, New York, Toronto: Longmans, Green & Co., 1951).

Baikie, J. *Egyptian Papyri And Papyrus-Hunting* (London: The Religious Tract Society, 1925).

Bell, H. Idris *Jews And Christians In Egypt* (London: The British Museum, 1924. Oxford University Press).

Benson, C. H. *A Guide For Bible Study*.

Bettenson, H. (Ed.) *Documents Of The Christian Church* (London: Oxford University Press, 1954).

Bruce, F. F. *Second Thoughts On The Dead Sea Scrolls* (London: The Paternoster Press, 1961).

Deissmann, A. *Light From The Ancient East. The New Testament Illustrated By Recently Discovered Texts Of The Graeco-Roman World*. Translated by Lionel R. M. Strachan. (London: Hodder & Stoughton, 1st edition, 1910).

Farrar, F. W. *The Messages Of The Books* (London: Macmillan & Co., 1884).

Furness, J. M. *Vital Words Of The Bible* (Grand Rapids, Michigan: Wm. B. Eerdmans Publishing Co., 1966).

Grenfell, B. P., and Hunt, A. S. (Translators & Editors) *The Oxyrhynchus Papyri.* Part II (London: Egypt Exploration Fund, Graeco-Roman Branch, 1899. University Press, Oxford).
—— Part IV (London: Egypt Exploration Fund, Graeco-Roman Branch, 1904. University Press, Oxford).

Head, E. D. *New Testament Life And Literature As Reflected In The Papyri* (Nashville, Tennessee: Broadman Press, 1952).
Hunt, A. S., and Smyly, J. G. (Editors) *The Tebtunis Papyri.* Volume III, Part I (London: Egypt Exploration Society, University of California Publications, Graeco-Roman Archaeology, Volume III. Humphrey Milford, Oxford University Press, 1933).

Milligan, G. *Selections From The Greek Papyri* (Cambridge: University Press, 1912).
Moulton, J. H. *From Egyptian Rubbish Heaps* (London: Charles H. Kelly, 1916).
Moulton, J. H., and Milligan, G. *The Vocabulary Of The Greek Testament* (London: Hodder & Stoughton, Ltd., 1957).

Tenney, M. C. *New Testament Times* (Grand Rapids, Michigan: Wm. B. Eerdmans Book Co., 1965).
Thompson, J. A. *The Bible And Archaeology* (Devon, England: The Paternoster Press, 1962).

Unger, M. F. *Archaeology And The New Testament* (Grand Rapids, Michigan: Zondervan Publishing House, 1962).

JOURNALS

Biblical Archaeologist (Published by the American Schools of Oriental Research).

Bulletin Of The American Schools Of Oriental Research

Bulletin Of The John Rylands Library, Manchester.

Journal Of Egyptian Archaeology (London : Egypt Exploration Fund).

Palestine Exploration Quarterly (London : Palestine Exploration Fund and British School of Archaeology in Jerusalem).

ABBREVIATIONS

B.G.U. *Aegyptische Urkunden aus den Koeniglichen Museen zu Berlin: Griechische Urkunden* I–VII, Berlin, 1895–1926.

J.E.A. *Journal of Egyptian Archaeology.*

Oxy. Pap. *The Oxyrhynchus Papyri*, ed. B. P. Grenfell and A. S. Hunt. Vols. I–VIII, London, 1898–1911.

P. Amh. *The Amherst Papyri* I and II. Ed. by B. P. Grenfell and A. S. Hunt. London, 1900–1.

P. Brit. Mus. *Greek Papyri in the British Museum.* Vols. I, II, ed. F. G. Kenyon; Vol. III, ed. F. G. Kenyon and H. I. Bell. London, 1893–1907.

P. Cairo Zen. *Catalogue Général des Antiquités Égyptiennes du Musée du Caire.* Nos. 59001–59531. *Zenon Papyri*, I, II, III. Ed. C. C. Edgar. Cairo, 1925–28.

P. Hib. *The Hibeh Papyri*, I. Ed. by B. P. Grenfell and A. S. Hunt. London, 1906.

P. Lond. *Greek Papyri in the British Museum.* Vols. I, II, III. Vols. IV, V, ed. H. I. Bell. London, 1893–1917.

P. Par. Paris Papyri in *Notices et Extraits* XVIII ii. Ed. Brunet de Presle. Paris, 1865.

P. Ryl. *Catalogue of the Greek Papyri in the John Rylands Library, Manchester* I, ed. A. S. Hunt; II, ed. J. de M. Johnson, V. Martin, and A. S. Hunt. Manchester, 1911–15.

Index of Persons, Places And Subjects

Index of Biblical References

123